www.hants.gov.uk/library

Hampshire County Council

Love YOUR LIBRARY

Tel: 0300 555 1387

Also by Leonard Cohen

THE FLAME

LEONARD
COHEN

Foreword by Adam Cohen

Edited by Robert Faggen and Alexandra Pleshoyano

CANONGATE

First published in Great Britain in 2018
by Canongate Books Ltd, 14 High Street, Edinburgh EH1 1TE

Published in the United States by Farrar, Straus and Giroux and in Canada by
Penguin Random House Canada Limited

canongate.co.uk

3

British Library Cataloguing-in-Publication Data
A catalogue record for this book is available on
request from the British Library

ISBN 978 1 78689 313 0

Text design by CS Richardson and Five Seventeen
Typeset in Optima by M&S Toronto

Printed and bound in Great Britain by Clays Ltd, Elcograf S.p.A.

The Flame

FOREWORD

This volume contains my father's final efforts as a poet. I wish he had seen it to completion—not because it would have been a better book in his hands, more realized and more generous and more shapely, or because it would have resembled him and the form he had in mind for this offering to his readers, more closely, but because it was what he was staying alive to do, his sole breathing purpose at the end. In the difficult period in which he was composing it, he would send 'do not disturb' emails to the few of us who would regularly drop by. He renewed his commitment to rigorous meditation so as to focus his mind through the acute pain of multiple compression fractures and the weakening of his body. He often remarked to me that, through all the strategies of art and living that he had employed during his rich and complicated life, he wished that he had more completely stayed steadfast to the recognition that writing was his only solace, his truest purpose.

My father, before he was anything else, was a poet. He regarded this vocation, as he records in the notebooks, as some "mission from G-d." (The hyphen indicating his reverence to the deity, his reluctance to write out the divine name even in English, is an old Jewish custom and is further evidence of the fidelity that he mixed with his freedom.) "Religion, teachers, women, drugs, the road, fame, money . . . nothing gets me high and offers relief from the suffering like blackening pages, writing." This statement of purpose was also a statement of regret: he offered his literary consecration as an explanation for what he felt was poor fatherhood, failed relationships, and inattention to his finances and health. I am reminded of one of his lesser-known songs (and one of my favorites): "I came so far for beauty, I left so much behind." But not far enough, apparently: in his view he hadn't left enough. And this book, he knew, was to be his last offering.

As a kid, when I would ask my dad for money to buy sweets at the corner store, he'd often tell me to search the pockets of his blazer for loose bills or change. Invariably, I would find a notebook while going through his pockets. Later in life, when I would ask him if he had a lighter or matches, I would open drawers and find pads of paper and notebooks. Once, when I asked him if he had any tequila, I was directed to the freezer, where I found a frosty, misplaced notebook. Indeed, to know my father was (among many other wondrous things) to know a man with papers, notebooks, and cocktail napkins—a distinguished handwriting on each—scattered (neatly) everywhere. They came from nightstands in hotels, or from 99 cent stores; the ones that were gilded, leather-bound, fancy, or otherwise had a look of importance, were never used. My father preferred humble vessels. By the early 1990s, there were storage lockers filled with boxes of his notebooks, notebooks containing a life of dedication to the thing that most defined the man. Writing was his reason for being. It was the fire he was tending to, the most significant flame he fueled. It was never extinguished.

There are many themes and words that repeat throughout my father's work: frozen, broken, naked, fire, and flame. On the back of the first album cover are (as he put it in a later song) the "flames that follow Joan of Arc." "Who by fire?" he famously asked, in a song about fate that wickedly made use of a Jewish prayer. "I lit a thin green candle to make you jealous of me." That candle was only the first of many kindlings. There are fires and flames, for creation and destruction, for heat and light, for desire and consummation, throughout his work. He lit the flames and he tended to them diligently. He studied and recorded their consequences. He was stimulated by their danger—he often spoke of other people's art as not having enough "danger," and he praised the "excitement of a thought that was in flames."

This fiery preoccupation lasted until the very end. "You want it darker, we kill the flame," he intoned on his last album, his parting album. He died on November 7, 2016. It feels darker now, but the flame was not killed. Each page of paper that he blackened was lasting evidence of a burning soul.

—Adam Cohen, February 2018

EDITORIAL NOTE

In the last months of his life, despite severe physical limitations, Leonard Cohen made selections for what would be his final volume of poems. *The Flame* presents this work in a format that his editors, Professors Robert Faggen and Alexandra Pleshoyano, and his long-time Canadian publisher believe reflects Leonard's intentions, based on the manuscript that he compiled, and using stylistic choices he made for previous books as a guide. Robert Faggen began the project working closely with Leonard, and Alexandra Pleshoyano joined to assist with completion of the editing in April 2017. Adam Cohen, Leonard's son, suggested the title.

Leonard provided clear instructions for the organization of the book, which was to contain written work and a generous sampling of his drawings and self-portraits. He envisioned three sections. The first section contains sixty-three poems that he had carefully selected, chosen from a trove of unpublished work that spans decades. Leonard was known to work on his poems for many years—sometimes many decades—before they were published; he considered these sixty-three poems completed works.

The second section contains the poems that became lyrics from his last four albums. All the lyrics for Leonard's songs begin as poems, and thus they can be appreciated as poems in their own right more than those of most songwriters. Notably, Leonard has published some of his lyrics as poems in the *New Yorker* prior to release of the album on which the song containing the lyrics appears. This was true most recently for "Steer Your Way," and previously for "A Street," "Almost Like the Blues," and "Going Home." In presenting the lyrics of Anjani Thomas' album *Blue Alert* (2006), produced by Leonard, and Leonard's *Old Ideas* (2012), *Popular Problems* (2014), and *You Want It Darker* (2016), we have followed the formatting which Leonard used in his book of selected poems and songs, *Stranger Music* (1993), which featured many lyrics. Careful readers will note differences between how these poems appear in *The Flame* and how the lyrics appear in the lyrics accompanying the albums.

The third section of the book presents a selection of entries from Leonard's notebooks, which he kept on a daily basis from his teenage years up until the last day of his life. Robert Faggen supervised the transcription of more than three thousand pages of notebooks that span six decades. Though Leonard participated in the selection of notebook entries for *The Flame*, he did not specify a final order. It would be challenging—if not impossible—to proceed chronologically because Leonard would often work in the same notebooks over many years with various coloured inks showing the different entries. Leonard numbered the notebooks in a system that we do not understand. That said, we chose to follow the numerical order of the notebooks even if these are apparently not always chronological. These notebook selections include a variety of stanzas and lines—what Leonard once called "scraps"—and readers familiar with Leonard's work will often see entries that appear to be working drafts of poems and lyrics. No attempt has been made to form a definitive narrative between these notebooks, and the entries have been reproduced here as closely as possible to the way they appear in the notebooks themselves, with no attempts made to change punctuation or line breaks. In transcribing the notebook entries, we followed certain conventions, and the following symbols are used in listing variants: { } indicates a word or phrase written above or below the line; [?] indicates an illegible word or phrase; and *** indicates a break between notebook entries.

In addition to these three sections of the book, Leonard wished to publish his acceptance speech for the Prince of Asturias Award, given in Spain on October 21, 2011. Elsewhere we are including—courtesy of Leonard's friend and colleague, Peter Scott—one of Leonard's last email exchanges, written less than twenty-four hours before his passing.

Leonard had suggested that some of his self-portraits and drawings be included, a practice that he began in *Book of Longing* (2006). Since Leonard did not have the chance to make these selections, Alexandra Pleshoyano chose nearly seventy self-portraits from more than 370 that he created, along with twenty-four drawings from his artwork. Leonard also agreed that we could reproduce some of the notebook pages to illustrate the book; twenty such selections are included here.

Finally, a few notes on individual poems. The poem "Full Employment" is essentially a longer version of the poem "G-d Wants His Song." The similarity between the poem "The Lucky Night" and the poem "Drank A lot" is also worth noting. The poem "Undertow" was released as a song on Leonard's album *Dear Heather* (2004). The poem "Never Gave Nobody Trouble" was also released as a song on Leonard's live album *Can't Forget: A Souvenir of the Grand Tour* (2015). The poems "A Street" and "Thanks for the Dance" are presented in slightly different versions as lyrics in the second part of the book. Those familiar with the *Leonard Cohen Files* website, hosted by Jarkko Arjatsalo, will recognize a few poems, self-portraits, and drawings, which had been posted there with Leonard's permission.

Robert Faggen and Alexandra Pleshoyano
July 2018

POEMS

HAPPENS TO THE HEART

I was always working steady
But I never called it art
I was funding my depression
Meeting Jesus reading Marx
Sure it failed my little fire
But it's bright the dying spark
Go tell the young messiah
What happens to the heart

There's a mist of summer kisses
Where I tried to double-park
The rivalry was vicious
And the women were in charge
It was nothing, it was business
But it left an ugly mark
So I've come here to revisit
What happens to the heart

I was selling holy trinkets
I was dressing kind of sharp
Had a pussy in the kitchen
And a panther in the yard
In the prison of the gifted
I was friendly with the guard
So I never had to witness
What happens to the heart

I should have seen it coming
You could say I wrote the chart
Just to look at her was trouble
It was trouble from the start
Sure we played a stunning couple
But I never liked the part
It ain't pretty, it ain't subtle
What happens to the heart

Now the angel's got a fiddle
And the devil's got a harp
Every soul is like a minnow
Every mind is like a shark
I've opened every window
But the house, the house is dark
Just say Uncle, then it's simple
What happens to the heart

I was always working steady
But I never called it art
The slaves were there already
The singers chained and charred
Now the arc of justice bending
And the injured soon to march
I lost my job defending
What happens to the heart

3

I studied with this beggar
He was filthy he was scarred
By the claws of many women
He had failed to disregard
No fable here no lesson
No singing meadowlark
Just a filthy beggar blessing
What happens to the heart

I was always working steady
But I never called it art
I could lift, but nothing heavy
Almost lost my union card
I was handy with a rifle
My father's .303
We fought for something final
Not the right to disagree

Sure it failed my little fire
But it's bright the dying spark
Go tell the young messiah
What happens to the heart

June 24, 2016

failed
portrait

I DO

I do, I love you Mary
More than I can say
Cuz if I ever said it
They'd take us both away

They'd lock us up for nothing
And throw away the key
The world don't like us Mary
They're on to you and me

We got a minute Mary
Before they pull the plug
50 seconds maybe
You know that's not enough

30 seconds baby
Is all we got to love
And if they catch us laughing
They gonna rough us up

I do, I love you Mary
More than I can say
Cuz if I ever said it
They'd take us both away

They'd lock us up for nothing
And throw away the key
The world don't like us Mary
They're on to you and me

LAMBCHOPS

thinking of those lambchops
at Moishe's the other night

we all taste good to one another
most bodies are good to eat
even reptiles and insects

even the poisonous lutefisk of Norway
buried in the dirt a million years before serving
and the poisonous blowfish of Japan
can be prepared
    to insure reasonable risks
at the table

if the crazy god did not want us to eat one another
why make our flesh so sweet

I heard it on the radio
a happy rabbit at the rabbit farm
saying to the animal psychic

don't be sad
it's lovely here
they're so good to us

we're not the only ones
said the rabbit
    comforting her

everyone gets eaten
as the rabbit said
to the animal psychic

2006

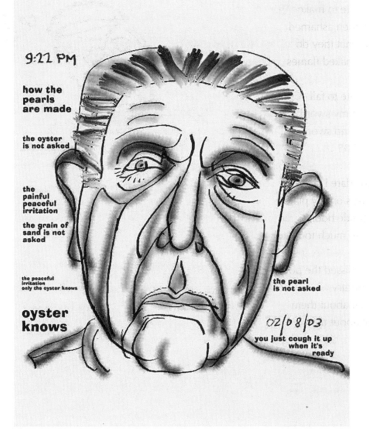

NO TIME TO CHANGE

No time to change
The backward look
It's much too late
My gentle book

Too late to make
The men ashamed
For what they do
With naked flames

Too late to fall
Upon my sword
I have no sword
It's 2005

How dare I care
What's on my plate
O gentle book
You're much too late

You missed the point
Of poetry
It's all about them
Not about me

careless is the way to go

I DIDN'T KNOW

I knew that I was weak
I knew that you were strong
I did not dare to kneel
Where I did not belong

And if I meant to touch
Your beauty with my hand
Then come the boils and blood
Which I would understand

You tore your knees apart
The loneliness revealed
That drew this unborn heart
From chains that would not yield

But weakened by your exercise
You fell against my soul
The stricken soul the mind denies
Until you make it whole

So I can love your beauty now
Though seeming from afar
Until my neutral world allow
How intimate you are

Sometimes it gets so lonely
I don't know what to do
I'd trade my stash of boredom
For a little hit of you

I didn't know
I didn't know
I didn't know
How much you needed me

I CAN'T TAKE IT ANYMORE

O apple of the world
we weren't married on the surface
we were married at the core
I can't take it anymore

surely there must be
a limit for the rich
and a hope unto the poor
I can't take it anymore

and the lies that they tell
about G-d
as if they owned the store
I can't take it anymore

UNDERTOW

I set out one night
When the tide was low
There were signs in the sky
But I did not know
I'd be caught in the grip
Of the undertow

And ditched on a beach
Where the sea hates to go
With a child in my arms
And a chill in my soul
And my heart the shape
Of a begging bowl

12

looking
for a
good
time,
sailor
?

Dec
23
'05

ON RARE OCCASIONS

On rare occasions
the power was given me
to send waves of emotion
through the world.
These were impersonal events,
over which I had no control.
I climbed on the outdoor stage
as the sun was going down
behind the Tower of Toledo
and the people did not let me go
until the middle of the night.
All of us,
the musicians, the audience,
were dissolved in gratitude.
There was nothing but
the starry darkness,
the smell of fresh cut hay,
and a hand of wind caressing
every single forehead.
I don't even remember the music.
A wide unison whispering arose
which I didn't understand.
When I left the stage
I asked the promoter
what they were saying.
He said they were chanting:
to-re-ro, to-re-ro
A young woman drove me back to the hotel,
a flower of the race.
All the windows were rolled down.
It was a ride free from error.
I could not feel the road
or the pull of destination.
We didn't speak
and there was no question of her
entering the lobby,
or climbing to my room.
Only recently
I remembered that drive of long ago,
and since then,
I need to be weightless
But I never am.

MY LAWYER

My lawyer tells me not to worry
Says that junk has killed the revolution
Leads me to the penthouse window
Tells me of his plan
To counterfeit the moon

1978

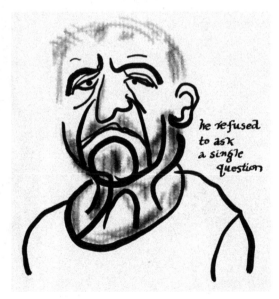

he refused
to ask
a single
question

I CAN'T BREAK THE CODE

I can't break the code
Of our frozen love
It's too late to know
What the password was

I reach for the past
Keep coming up short
And everything feels
Like a last resort

When she is not calling you

Tho' we've called it quits
And there's nothing left
Still I hear my lips
Make these promises

Though we've squandered the truth
And there's little left
We can still sweep the room
We can still make the bed

When the world is false
I won't say it's true
When the darkness calls
I will go with you

In a time of shame
In the great Alarm
When they call your name
We'll go arm in arm

I'M LOOKING AT THE FLAG

I'm looking at the flag
My hand against my heart
If only we could win
(One of) these wars we like to start

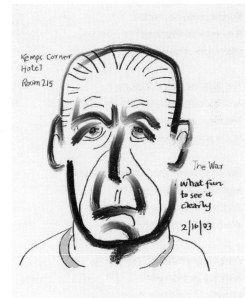

Kemps Corner
Hotel
Room 215

The War
what fun
to see it
clearly

2/16/03

THE LUCKY NIGHT!!!!! SUNDAY MARCH 7, 2004

Let's say that on that lucky night
I found my house in order
and I could slip away unseen
tho' burning with desire

Escaping down a secret stair
I cross into the forest
the night is dark but I am safe—
my house at last in order

But luck or not, I do it right
and no one sees me leaving
hidden, blind and secret night—
my heart the only beacon

But O that beacon lights my way
more surely than the sun,
and She is waiting for me there—
of all and all, the only One

And then the night commands me
to enter in Her side
and be as Adam is to Eve
before they need divide

So I can show Her what's been kept
for Her and Her alone—
a secret place that Love had left
before the world was born

Her nipples underneath My hand
Her fingers in My hair—
a forest crying from the dead
and fragrance everywhere

And from the wall a grazing wind
weightless and serene
wounds Me as I part Her lips
and wounds Us in between

And fastened here, surrendered to
My Lover and My Lover,
We spread and drown as lilies do—
forever and forever

HE SAYS HE WANTS TO KILL US

he says he wants to kill us
he says it very often
just let him know you love him
his attitude will soften

let's wait a little while
let's wait a little longer
the enemy is gaining strength
let's wait until he's stronger

ROSHI SAID

1.
Roshi said:

Jikan san, there's something I want you to
know

yes, Roshi

you are the worst student I've ever had

2.
I disappeared for ten years.
When I came back to Los Angeles
Roshi invited me for dinner.
After dinner Roshi wanted to see me
alone.

Roshi said:

When you left half of me died.

I said:

I don't believe you.

Roshi said:

Good answer.

3.
During Roshi's sex scandal (he was 105)
my association with Roshi
was often mentioned in the newspaper
reports.

Roshi said:

I give you lots of trouble.

I said:

Yes, Roshi, you give me
lots of trouble.

Roshi said:

I should die.

I said:

It won't help.

Roshi didn't laugh.

IF THERE WERE NO PAINTINGS

If there were no paintings in the world,
Mine would be very important.
Same with my songs.
Since this is not the case, let us make haste to get in line,
Well towards the back.
Sometimes I would see a woman in a magazine
Humiliated in the technicolour glare.
I would try to establish her
In happier circumstances.
Sometimes a man.
Sometimes living persons sat for me.
May I say to them again:
Thank you for coming to my room.
I also loved the objects on the table
Such as candlesticks and ashtrays
And the table itself.
From a mirror on my desk
In the very early morning
I copied down
Hundreds of self-portraits
Which reminded me of one thing or another.
The Curator has called this exhibition
Drawn to Words.
I call my work
Acceptable Decorations.

JAN 15, 2007 SICILY CAFÉ

And now that I kneel
At the edge of my years
Let me fall through the mirror of love

And the things that I know
Let them drift like the snow
Let me dwell in the light that's above

In the radiant light
Where there's day and there's night
And truth is the widest embrace

That includes what is lost
Includes what is found
What you write and what you erase

And when will my heart break open
When will my love be born
In this scheme of unspeakable suffering
Where even the blueprint is torn

DEPRIVED

Deprived of Sahara's company
I looked around the room
and spied her purse
at the foot of the chair
I went through every item
in a little notebook
written with an eyebrow pencil
I found the very poem
which you are reading now—
the writing smudged
but word for word:
"Straighten up, little warrior," it ended
"It's not as though you
wasted your life
by loving me."

no gifts
this morning
no free samples

doesn't even
look like me

want to write
a "love song"
for the tread-
mill
and the rowing
machine

baby baby what you do to me
baby baby what you do to me

1/28/03

DIMENSIONS OF LOVE

Sometimes I hear you stop abruptly
and change your direction
and start towards me
I hear it as a kind of rustling
My heart leaps up to greet you
to greet you in the air
to take you back home
to resume our long life together
Then I remember
the uncrossable dimensions of love
and I prepare myself
for the consequences of memory
and longing
but memory with its list of years
turns gracefully aside
and longing kneels down
like a calf
in the straw of amazement
and for the moment that it takes
to keep your death alive
we are refreshed
in each other's timeless company

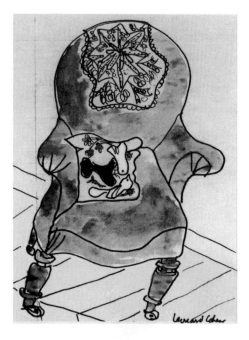

FULL EMPLOYMENT
For V.R. (1978–2000)

Vanessa called
all the way from Toronto.
She said that I
could count on her
if ever I was down and out.
After I hung up the phone
I played
the six-holed wooden flute
she gave me
on the occasion of our parting.
I figured out the fingering
and I played it better
than I had ever done.
Tears came out of my eyes
because of the sound,
and the recollection
of her extraordinary beauty
which no one could avoid,
and because she said
a song had gone missing,
and I had been selected,
out of all the unemployed,
I had been selected
to recover it.

I see you in windows
that open so wide
there's nothing beyond them,
and nothing inside.

You take off your sandals
you shake out your hair,
your beauty dismantled
and worn everywhere.

The story's been written.
The letter's been sealed.
You gave me a lily,
but now it's a field.

you gave me
a lily
but now
it's a
field

you kick off your sandals
you shake out your hair
it's torn where you're dancing
it's torn every where

it's torn
on the right
and it's torn
on the left
and it's torn
in the centre
which few
can accept

come gather the pieces
all scattered and lost
the lie in what's holy
the light in
what's not

Montreal

I HEAR THE TRAFFIC

I hear the traffic
On the Main
Love my coffee
Love Charmaine

Another day
To rise and fall
Make a buck
Start and stall

I love Charmaine
Her heart is kind
I'm still a fool
She doesn't mind

Her eyes are grey
But when I'm mean
Her eyes display
A shade of green

February 26, 2000

HOMAGE TO MORENTE

When I listen to Morente
I know what I must do
When I listen to Morente
I don't know what to do
When I listen to Morente
My life becomes too shallow
To swim in
I dig but I can't go down
I reach but I can't go up
When I listen to Morente
I know I have betrayed
The solemn promise
The solemn promise that justified
All my betrayals
When I listen to Morente
The alibi of my throat is rejected
The alibi of my gift is overthrown
With six impeccable threads of scorn
My guitar turns away from me
And I want to give everything back
But no one wants it
When I listen to Morente
I surrender to my feeble imagination
Which itself has surrendered long ago
To the Great Voice of the Taverns
And the Families and the Hills
When I listen to Morente
I am humbled but not humiliated

I go with him now
Out of the darkness of what I could not be
Into the darkness of the song I could not sing
The song that hungers for an earthquake
The song that hungers for religion
Then I hear him begin the great ascent
I hear Morente's Aleluya
His thundering murderous serene Aleluya
I hear it rise to the impossible occasion
And pierce the ordinary ambiguities
With the sharpened horns
Of his own inconceivable ambiguities

the background singers

His cry his perfect word pitched against
The baffled contradictions of the heart
Wrestling them embracing them
Strangling them with a jealous conjugal desperation
And he hangs it there beneath his voice
Above all the broken ceilings
The disappointed sky
His voice escaped from the mud of hope
And the blood of the throat
And the strict training of the cante
And he hangs it there
The Kingdom of Morente
Which he does not enter as Morente
But as the great impersonal anointed Voice
Of the Taverns and the Families and the Hills
And he takes us there
By the bleeding finger by the throat by the soiled lapel
Takes what's left of us
To his Kingdom
the Kingdom of Poverty he himself established
The only place we want to be
Or ever wanted to be
Where we can breathe the childhood air
The unborn air
Where we are nobody at last
Where we cannot go without him
Long live Enrique Morente
Long live the Family Morente
The dancers the singers
The disciples of the Taverns and the Families and the Hills

the dazed middle self

the inner self is clear and doubtless
the outer self is confident and highly functional
I show you the dazed middle self - the DMS

2/6/03

Room 215
Hotel
Kemps Corner

****

HOMAGE TO ROSENGARTEN

If you have a wall, a bare wall in your house
All the walls in my house are bare
And I love the bare walls
The only thing I would put up
On one of my beloved bare walls
Not beloved
It doesn't need beloved
It doesn't need an adjective
The wall is fine as it is
But I would put up a Rosengarten
A Rosengarten produced with a wooden
Comb and black ink
Going nowhere forever in a swirl of indelible parallel curves
Is it a letter or a woman?
It is another perfect startling black letter in a word
Among hundreds of words
In a continuing Rosengarten epic that celebrates
Mankind's holy and relentless desire for itself
Your heart is the same as the white paper
Upon which the woman is so carefully splashed
Both need her in order to become significant
If you had a vast white wall
And if you hung hundreds of his commanding women in a row
You would not have to study the calligraphy
For very long
To understand and to forgive yourself
For falling in love so often
And for championing our mysterious and radiant race
And it would silence whatever foolish argument
About beauty
You had been tricked into embracing

And it is the same with a piece of furniture
I have one or two wooden tables
That I bought for a song long ago
I've polished them for years
And I don't want anything on them
Except elbows a plate and a glass
But I have a Rosengarten on one of them

Because a Rosengarten celebrates the wood it stands on
Because it is made with the same mind
That made the table a hundred years ago
The mind of honour and skill and modesty
That patiently manifests an artifact
Of unutterable usefulness
You would have to live with a Rosengarten
To know how useful it is
As useful as a table or a wall
To serve your helplessness
To locate your "wrecked life" in a room
You have forgotten to explore
Just as there is no extra word in a great poem
In a Rosengarten
There is no extra volume
There is no gesture, no conceit, no winking eye
Soliciting a compliment
It is as it is
Respectful of the tradition from which it arises
But independent of it too
It stands there surrounded by the room
Establishing second after second
New alarming original friendships with the air and the light
Which the room so deeply needs
To irrigate and refresh your struggle

And if you have a garden or an acre
And you want it to flourish
Place a number of Rosengartens here and there
His great commanding Asherahs
The streamlined female presence
Which men and women sought and worshipped
In the "high places" of the Bible
And still do today
As we walk hand in hand
Through the bewildering and shabby insignificance
Of our official corrected public and private daily lives
And here She is:
Fully born from herself
Urgent and accommodating
A thrust of polished energy that does not cut the air
But softens it and ignites it softly

Offered up on a simple stone staircase
Which in itself is a masterpiece of escalating harmony
Offered to the mystery of beauty
Which no one dare explain
Offered up for the secret reasons
Which are known to all
Offered up in the usual conditions of distress
And the deep inner certainty of perfection
And now your garden
Does not need reminding

I'M ALWAYS THINKING OF A SONG

I'm always thinking of a song
For Anjani to sing
It will be about our lives together
It will be very light or very deep
But nothing in between
I will write the words
And she will write the melody
I won't be able to sing it
Because it will climb too high
She will sing it beautifully
And I'll correct her singing
And she'll correct my writing
Until it is better than beautiful
Then we'll listen to it
Not often
Not always together
But now and then
For the rest of our lives

ROSHI'S POEM

Whenever I hear
The edgeless sound
In the deep night
O Mother!
I find you again.

Whenever I stand
Beneath the light
Of the seamless sky
O Father!
I bow my head.

The sun goes down
Our shadows dissolve
The pine trees darken
O Darling!
We must go home.

Tr. Leonard Cohen

KANYE WEST IS NOT PICASSO

Kanye West is not Picasso
I am Picasso
Kanye West is not Edison
I am Edison
I am Tesla
Jay-Z is not the Dylan of anything
I am the Dylan of anything
I am the Kanye West of Kanye West
The Kanye West
Of the great bogus shift of bullshit culture
From one boutique to another
I am Tesla
I am his coil
The coil that made electricity soft as a bed
I am the Kanye West Kanye West thinks he is
When he shoves your ass off the stage
I am the real Kanye West
I don't get around much anymore
I never have
I only come alive after a war
And we have not had it yet

March 15, 2015

OLD FRIENDS

An old man tells his friend (over the telephone) that
he is going to shule that evening. It is a broken-
down shule in a hostile black neighbourhood in Los
Angeles. There is never even half a minyan (ten
men). The worshippers are old, the prayers are badly
spoken, the place is draughty and full of shabbiness
and lumbago. The old man is inviting his friend to
laugh with him over the wreck of a failed spiritual
adventure, an adventure in which both of them once
cherished the highest hopes. But his friend does not
laugh. His friend becomes Nachmanides, the
Bodhidharma, and St. Paul all rolled into one religious
accountant. "You should not have told me that you
were going to shule. You lose all the merit you
would have gained had you remained silent." What?
Merit? Silence? Who is the old man talking to?
That's rich. His friend is rebuking him for boasting
about his piety, but he lets it go (sort of). After
they say goodnight, the old man puts on his robes,
which don't fit so well now that he's given up
smoking. There is an almost full bottle of Prozac on
his night-table. He bought the refill a couple of
months ago, but almost immediately stopped taking
the pill. It didn't work. Hardly anything works
anymore. You can't even tell your friend (over the
telephone) about your lumbago without getting a
lecture. At least his dentist didn't reproach him
when he went back last week. After two years'
absence and a rotting mouth which everyone
(dentist, assistant, himself) could smell when the
scraping started. His dentist was an old man too.
"Let's tackle this," was all he said. The old man ties
the strings of his robe and puts on all the lights in
the house (so he won't get robbed again). He drives
into the war zone, locking his doors on the way, and
he parks in the courtyard of the zendo (it isn't really
a shule). Eunice is there. She's been there for
twenty-five years. "At my age," I heard her say the
other night, something about how easily she catches

cold now. Koyo is there. I forget his Christian name.
The fingers of his right hand are swollen from a cat
bite. Infected. He fumbles with the incense. Eunice
sneezes and coughs and hacks. A police helicopter
drowns out the chanting. The place is freezing. Just
the three of us. The fluff is coming out of the
cushion, just like the juice is coming out of this
story, and I'm not pissed off at you anymore either,
Steve. And what is more, old friend, you have a
point. You have a point.

1985

Bodhidharma
brought Zen
to the West
but I
got rid of it

Sheraton Tel Aviv
12th floor
grey and white
the windy sea

THE APPARENT TURBULENCE

You were the last young woman
to look at me that way
When was it
sometime between 9/11 and the tsunami
You looked at my belt
and then I looked down at my belt
you were right
it wasn't bad
then we resumed our lives.
I don't know about yours
but mine is curiously peaceful
behind the apparent turbulence
of litigation and advancing age

WATCHING THE NATURE CHANNEL

the boredom of God
is heartbreaking
fiddle fiddle fiddle

the importance
of a previous
existence as
a fish
has been
exaggerated

THE CREATURE

the creature who says
"me" and "mine"
need not bend down in shame—
along with lakes and mountains
the ego is created
and divine

THE INDIAN GIRL

You're waiting. You've always been waiting. It's nothing new. You've waited whenever you wanted anything, and you were waiting when the kettle sang to the canary and the Indian girl let you make love to her secretly before she died in a car accident. You were waiting for your wife to become sweet, you were waiting for your body to become thin and muscular, and the girl from India, in her apartment on Mackay Street, she said, *Leonard, you've been waiting for me all afternoon, especially when we were all listening to the canary in your wife's kitchen, that's when it really got to you, the three of us standing in front of the cage, the kettle whistling and our great expectations for the canary, the song that was going to lift the three of us out of the afternoon, out of the winter—that's when the waiting was too much for you, that's when I understood how deeply and impersonally you desired me, and that's when I decided to invite you into my arms.* Supposing she said this to herself. And then I drove her home and she invited me up to her apartment and she did not resist my profound impersonal affection for her dark unknown person, and she saw how general, how neutral, how relentlessly impersonal was this man's aching for her—and she took me to the green Salvation Army couch, among the student furniture, she took me because she was going to die in two weeks in a car accident on the Laurentian highway, she took me in one of her last embraces, because she saw how simple I would be to comfort, and I was so grateful to be numbered among her last generous activities on this earth. And I went back to my wife, my young wife, the one who would never thaw, who would bear me children, who would hate me for one good reason or another all the days of her life, who would know a couple of my friends a little too well. We stood, the three of us, listening to the duet of the canary and the kettle, the steam clouding the windows of our kitchen on Esplanade, and the Montreal winter shutting everything down but the heart of hope. Mara was her name, and she came to visit us, as we made visits in those days, driving through the snow to meet someone new.

44

1980

MARY FULL OF GRACE

You step out of the shower
Oh so cool and clean
Smelling like a flower
From a field of green
The world is burning Mary
It's hollow dark and mean

I love to hear you laugh
It takes the world away
I live to hear you laugh
I don't even have to pray
But now the world is coming back
It's coming back to stay

Stand beside me Mary
We have no time to waste
The water's not like water now
It has a bitter taste
Stand beside me Mary
Mary full of grace

I know you have to leave me
The clock is ticking loud
I know it's time to leave me
The time has come around
My heart has turned to weaponry
That's why my head is bowed

Stand beside me Mary
We have no time to waste
The animal is bleeding
And the flower is disgraced
Stand beside me Mary
Mary full of grace

THE LOS ANGELES TIMES

The *Los Angeles Times*
is going to be read
by a man named Carlo.
He will die carrying his wife
(who cannot use her legs)
to the bathroom.
I will sit in the sun
writing about them.
My dog will die,
my hamster, my turtle
my white rat, my tropical fish
my Moroccan squirrel.
My mother and father will die,
and so will my friends Robert and
        Derek.
Sheila will die
in her new life without me.
My high school teacher will die,
Mr. Waring.
Frank Scott will die,
leaving a freer Canada behind him.
Glenn Gould will die
in the midst of his glory.
Marshall McLuhan will die
having altered several meanings.
Milton Acorn will die
just after putting out his cigar
on my carpet.
Lester B. Pearson will die
wearing the bow tie of Winston
        Churchill.
Bliss Carman will die
before I learned about his loneliness.
The Group of Seven will die
having made some places famous
where I used to camp,
where I pitched my tent
and gutted fish
in the loving sight of Anne of Carlyle.

My brother-in-law,
the most eminent of all Frequent Flyers,
he will die a True Son of the Law
and leave my sister 2 million miles.
It doesn't matter
that all these deaths occurred
long before I prophesized them.
History will overlook
the tiny glitches in sequential time
and concentrate
rather
on my relentless concern
with matters mostly Canadian.

Terrace of Medical Building,
November 15, 1999

the truth
feels good

46

47

YOU WANT TO STRIKE BACK AND YOU CAN'T

You want to strike back and you can't
And you want to help but you can't
And the gun won't shoot
And the dynamite won't explode
And the wind is blowing the other way
And no one can hear you
And death is everywhere
And you're dying anyhow
And you're tired of the war
And you can't explain one more time

You can't explain anymore
And you're stuck behind your house
Like an old rusted truck
That will never haul another load

And you're not leading your life
You're leading someone else's life
Someone you don't know or like
And it's ending soon
And it's too late to begin again
Armed with what you know now

And all your stupid charities
Have armed the poor against you
And you're not who you wanted to be
Not remotely he or she
How am I going to get out of this
The untidy mess the untidiness
Never to be clean again or free
Soiled by gossip and publicity

You're tired and it's over
And you can't do any more
That's what this silence
That's what this song is for

And you can't explain anymore
And you can't dig in
Because the surface is like steel
And all your fine emotions
Your subtle insights
Your famous understanding
Evaporate into stunning
(To you) irrelevance

I don't remember when
I wrote this
It was long before 9/11

WHEN YOU WAKE UP

When you wake up into the panic
and the tulips from Ralph's
have almost had it,
why don't you change the water
and cut the stems,
maybe find a vase a little taller
to help them stand up straight?
When you wake up into the panic
and the Devil's almost got you
to throw yourself off the cliffs of religion,
why don't you lie down
in front of the ferocious traffic
of your daily life
and get creamed by some of the details?

December 13, 1993

So good to wake up with you, beloved

January 23
2003

WHEN DESIRE RESTS

You know I'm looking at you
you know what I'm thinking
you know you're interested
I am very skillful
you will forget that I am old
unless you want to remember it
unless you want to see
what happens to desire
how free it becomes
how shamelessly involved in love
for every woman
                and her stockings.
When desire rests,
it is signaled by two people
faraway on a green blanket
(or is it the flowers of moss);
two people waving from a distance
stretched out like things
                that have to dry
with tender smiles on their
                little round faces;
waving at desire
as it rests in the foreground
foothill-shaped, peaceful,
devoted as a dog made of tears.

WHAT IS COMING 2.16.03

what is coming
ten million people
in the street
cannot stop
what is coming
the American Armed Forces
cannot control
the President
of the United States
      and his counselors
cannot conceive
initiate
command
      or direct
everything
you do
or refrain from doing
will bring us
to the same place
the place we don't know

your anger against the war
your horror of death
your calm strategies
your bold plans
to rearrange
      the middle east
to overthrow the dollar
to establish
      the 4th Reich
to live forever
to silence the Jews
to order the cosmos
to tidy up your life
to improve religion
they count for nothing
you have no understanding
of the consequences
of what you do
oh and one more thing
you aren't going to like
what comes after
      America

what is coming
ten million people
in the street
cannot stop

what is coming
the American Armed Forces
cannot control
the President
of the United States
           and his counselors
cannot conceive
initiate
command
         or direct

everything
you do
or refrain from doing
will bring us
to the same place
the place we don't know

your anger against the war
your horror of death
your calm strategies
your bold plans
to rearrange
           the middle east
to overthrow the dollar
to establish
           the 4th Reich
to live forever
to silence the Jews
to order the cosmos
to tidy up your life
to improve religion
they count for nothing

you have no understanding
of the consequences
of what you do

oh and one more thing
you aren't going to like
what comes after
           America

WHAT I DO

It's not that I like
to live in a hotel
in a place like India
and write about G-d
and run after women
It seems to be
what I do

SCHOOL DAYS

I headed the school
I was the school head
John was the arms
Peggy was the asshole
and Jennifer the toes.
I loved the asshole best.

In my striped football sweater
and in my v-neck hockey shirt
I was a sight.
No wonder Peggy fell
under my influence.
Until the accident.
Then I lost her.

Flags wave and banners ripple.
All is lost for the visiting team.
There I am in a bad seat
scowling at our victory.
I cannot take my eyes off
her little bouncing skirt.
I'm talking about the cheerleader
named Peggy.
That was forty-seven years ago.
The Past.
I never think about The Past
but sometimes
The Past thinks about me
and sits down
ever so lightly on my face—

And me and Peggy
and John and Jennifer,
our scarves in the wind,
we're speeding
in the family roadster
to someone's house
in Nantucket
and I can walk again.

with a great sense of relief
(prompted by a study of the lower face)
he begins to experience the sweet
anonymity in the blessed order
of all withering things

September 2003
Los Angeles

THE FLOWERS HATE US

the flowers hate us
the animals pray for our death
as soon as i found out
i murdered my dog

now i knew what they were up to
the daisy the iris the rose
why there was no peace among men
why nothing worked

there is no going back
throw out your friend's bouquet
kill the animals all of them
but don't eat their meat

It will be
worse than
wax

now that i know what they're thinking
their sex organs in the air
their stinking fur
and their tug at the heart

what they would do to us if they won

how great it will be without them
just getting on with our short lives
which are longer than theirs
and until now, sadder

the flowers hate us
the animals pray for us to die
as soon as i found out
i murdered my dog

They hate us
They pray for us to die
Wake up America
Murder your dog

UNBIBLICAL

I thought I'd get away
But now I have to stay
I think I'd better say:
As usual

It wasn't up to me
I heard the stern decree
I wasn't meant to be
That beautiful

Some people catch the bus
They're luckier than us
In spite of all the fuss
They're credible

They want to get on board
They don't like to be ignored
They're children of the lord
They're terrible

You've heard this all before
I had some but they had more
I was rotten to the core
But merciful

And that was my mistake
I didn't kill the snake
I gave the snake a break
Unbiblical

WINTER ON MOUNT BALDY

It's winter on Mount Baldy
The monks are shoveling snow
It's swinging free, the Gateless Gate
But no one seems to go

It's cold and dark and dangerous
And slippery as a lie
Nobody wants to be here
And me, I'd rather die

All the food is second-hand
And everyone complains
The priceless shit of yesteryear
Is frozen in the drains

It's winter on Mount Baldy
The monks are shoveling snow
It's swinging free, the Gateless Gate
But no one seems to go

Forget about your purity
Your blemishes and stains
You want to climb Mount Baldy
You're going to need your chains

It's cold and dark and dangerous
And slippery as a lie
Nobody wants to be here
Some say they'd rather die

You had the Himalayas
And the great Tibetan plains
You want to take Mount Baldy
You're going to need your chains

August 21, 2015

this way is really the best way
I'm sorry to say
whatever you have in mind
won't do anymore
I base this on over 50 yrs
of close observation
this is the best way now
this is comfortable
this is home

so much for you
my dear colonel
you never did figure out
how to deal with what
is truly unimportant

DOESN'T MATTER

it doesn't matter darling,
it really doesn't matter,
and i don't say
it doesn't matter,
in order to hurt you into feeling:
that it DOES MATTER,
that it REALLY DOES MATTER.
not at all,
not at all.
i stand beside you
in the midst of this vast enterprise
of human activity and desire,
deafened by the noise
of my own heart,
twisted by an appetite
for justice and for peace,
and i look at you,
the one i tried to love,
the one who tried to love me,
and it comes to us
from the place where we began,
the place where we will end,
a voice that includes
your voice, and my voice,
and we are
gathered together,
we are born together,

and we die in each other's arms,
and it is heard as a mighty voice,
or a gentle voice,
a whispered voice,
or a thundered voice,
above all,
the voice that we most
desperately
long to hear,
it is the voice that can forgive us,
and it says,
it doesn't matter
darling,
it is the truth,
the truth of all forgiving.
listen now. listen from
the wreck of your baffled love.
it is the truth,
the very truth
of all forgiving.
it doesn't matter darling.
it really doesn't matter.

GRATEFUL

The huge mauve jacaranda tree
down the street on South Tremaine
in full bloom
                    two stories high
It made me so happy
And then
the first cherries of the season
at the Palisades Farmers Market
                    Sunday morning
"What a blessing!"
I exclaimed to Anjani
And then the samples on waxed paper
of the banana cream cake
and the coconut cream cake
        I am not a lover of pastry
but I recognized the genius of the baker
and touched my hat to her
                    A slight chill in the air
seemed to polish the sunlight
and confer the status of beauty
                    to every object I beheld
Faces bosoms fruits pickles green eggs
newborn babies
                    in clever expensive harnesses
I am so grateful
to my new anti-depressant

he has found his way
and he has begun

to smile

he smiles at
everyone

he is a regular

Father Teresa

ANTIQUE SONG

Too old, too old to play the part,
Too old, God only knows!
I'll keep the little silver heart,
The red and folded rose.

And in the arms of someone strong
You'll have what we had none.
I'll finish up my winter song
For you. It's almost done.

But oh! the kisses that we kissed,
That swept me to the shore
Of seas where hardly I exist,
Except to kiss you more.

I have the little silver heart,
The red and folded rose.
The one you gave me at the start,
The other at the close.

He waited for you all night long.
Go run to him, go run.
I'll finish up my winter song,
For you. It's almost done.

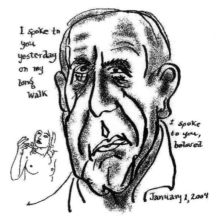

I spoke to you yesterday on my long walk

I spoke to you, beloved

January 1, 2004

ELEVATOR MIRRORS

My father had a mustache,
But not his father or his brothers
I am very tempted

In the new hotels
The elevators are often so dark
The mirrors are useless
(Like this one)

I don't want to go anywhere
I've been to the Acropolis (1959)
I sat on the old stones
And was photographed with a woman
    (1970)
Who troubled my life
From then until now (2008)

Dying in reasonable circumstances
Is mostly what I hope for
But here I am on the road
Far from reasonable circumstances

There is a woman I like
She is young and beautiful and kind
And cannot sing
But she wants to be a singer

I used to keep a full picture of her
Hidden on my laptop
Then I thought:
I can't do this again
And I dragged it (reluctantly)
To the little trash basket
Which I did not empty for quite a while

In the elevator
Of the Manchester Malmaison Hotel
I have to put on reading glasses
To find the button for my floor
The corridors are dark purple
Lit with pinpoint lights
Bass-heavy hip-hop
Dooming the generation
From hidden speakers
You squint to find your door

(The entire enterprise
Of travel and lodging
Now pitched
As a dangerous erotic adventure)

I'm no one to say
Who can or can't be a singer
God knows my own credentials
Were not extensive
It was Good Fortune
As success always is
Period

(A really lovely person
I don't have to introduce
To anyone at Sony)

LISTEN TO THE HUMMINGBIRD

Listen to the hummingbird
Whose wings you cannot see
Listen to the hummingbird
Don't listen to me.

Listen to the butterfly
Whose days but number three
Listen to the butterfly
Don't listen to me.

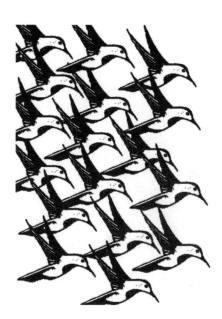

Listen to the one in charge
Who studies your ID
Listen to the one in charge
Don't listen to me.

Listen to the sovereign heart
Resign its sovereignty
Listen to the sovereign heart
Don't listen to me.

Listen to the mind of God
Which doesn't need to be
Listen to the mind of God
Don't listen to me.

I THINK I'LL BLAME

I think I'll blame
my death on you
but I don't know you
well enough
if I did
we'd be married now

For the full enjoyment
(and I promise you
there is such a thing)
it is not enough to read
between the lines
that is child's play
and we are not that fond
of children

One day
you will pick up this book
as if
for the first time
and say to yourself:
I don't know how the guy
pulled it off

Line after line
rises from my predicament—
the nerve, you'll say
the fucking nerve

And strengthened by
your indifference
to the matter
not to mention
the entire question of the
past

You will recall
how good you were to me
how good I was to you

And standing at some
commanding place
like a window or a cliff
you will know
the full enjoyment

Hotel Kemps Corner
Room 215
9:36 PM

yes
always somewhat
off balance

but peaceful
in his work
peaceful
in his vertigo

an old man
with his pen
deeply familiar
with his
predicament

MY GUITAR STOOD UP TODAY

My guitar stood up today
and leaped into my arms to play
a Spanish tune for dancers proud
to stamp their feet and cry aloud
against the fate that bends us down
beneath the thorny bloody crown
of sickness, age, and paranoid
delusions I, for one, cannot avoid

MY CAREER

So little to say
So urgent
to say it

NEVER GAVE NOBODY TROUBLE

i couldn't pay the mortgage
and i broke my baby's heart
i couldn't pay the mortgage
and i broke my baby's heart
never gave nobody trouble
but it ain't too late to start

don't want to break no window
don't want to burn no car
don't want to break no window
don't want to burn your car
you got a right to all your riches
but you let it go too far

you sail the mighty ocean
in a yacht designed for you
you sail the mighty ocean
in a yacht designed for you
but the ocean's thick with garbage
you ain't going to make it through

never gave nobody trouble
i'm a law and order man
never gave nobody trouble
i'm a law and order man
never gave nobody trouble
but you know damn well I can

if I
catch
you
making
fun
of me
I will
wash
your
face
with
snow

and
I will
be
sitting
on you

Sunday January
11th
2004

ORDINARY GUY WITH PROBLEMS

Ordinary guy with problems
You've seen him around
Some of the places you go
He's not caving in
Don't have to be nice to him
He knows where to get a drink
He can be alone
Ordinary guy with problems

DRANK A LOT

i drank a lot. i lost my job.
i lived like nothing mattered.
then you stopped, and came across
my little bridge of fallen answers.

i don't recall what happened next.
i kept you at a distance.
but tangled in the knot of sex
my punishment was lifted.

and lifted on a single breath—
no coming and no going—
o G-d, you are the only friend
i never thought of knowing.

your remedies beneath my hand
your fingers in my hair
the kisses on our lips began
that ended everywhere.

and now our sins are all confessed
our strategies forgiven
it's written that the law must rest
before the law is written.

and not because of what i'd lost
and not for what i'd mastered
you stopped for me, and came across
the bridge of fallen answers.

tho' mercy has no point of view
and no one's here to suffer
we cry aloud, as humans do:
we cry to one another.

And now it's one, and now it's two,
And now the whole disaster.
We cry for help, as humans do—
Before the truth, and after.

And Every Guiding Light Was Gone
And Every Teacher Lying—
There Was No Truth In Moving On—
There Was No Truth In Dying.

And Then The Night Commanded Me
To Enter In Her Side—
And Be As Adam Was To Eve
Before The Great Divide.

her remedies beneath my hand
her fingers in my hair—
and every mouth of hunger glad—
and deeply unaware.

and here i cannot lift a hand
to trace the lines of beauty,
but lines are traced, and beauty's glad
to come and go so freely.

and from the wall a grazing wind,
weightless and routine—
it wounds us as i part your lips
it wounds us in between.

and every guiding light was gone
and every sweet direction—
the book of love i read was wrong
it had a happy ending.

And Now There Is No Point Of View—
And Now There Is No Other—
We Spread And Drown As Lilies Do—
We Spread And Drown Forever.

You are my tongue, you are my eye,
My coming and my going.
O G-d, you let your sailor die
So he could be the ocean.

And when I'm at my hungriest
She takes away my tongue
And holds me here where hungers rest
Before the world is born.

And fastened here we cannot move
We cannot move forever
We spread and drown as lilies do—
From nowhere to the center.

Escaping through a secret gate
I made it to the border
And call it luck—or call it fate—
I left my house in order.

And now there is no point of view—
And now there is no other—
We spread and drown as lilies do—
We spread and drown forever.

Disguised as one who lived in peace
I made it to the border
Though every atom of my heart
Was burning with desire.

Sunday, March 7, 2004

IKKYU

Ikkyu
is not a monk,
not much of a poet,
and as a lover,
it's hit and run.
He'd need
a hundred years of America,
and a long shower
just to keep his hand in.

FLYING OVER ICELAND

over Reykjavik, the "smokey bay"
where W.H. Auden went
to discover the background
of all our songs,
where I myself was received
by the Mayor and the President
(600 miles an hour
30,000 feet
599 miles an hour
my old street number on Belmont Ave)
where I, a second-rater
by any estimation,
was honoured by the noblest
and handsomest people of the West
served with lobster
and strong drink,
and I never cared about eyes
but the eyes of the waitress
were so alarmingly mauve
that I fell into a trance
and ate the forbidden shellfish

G-D WANTS HIS SONG

Vanessa called
all the way from Toronto
she said that I
could count on her
if ever I was
down and out
After I put the phone down
i played the six-holed wooden flute
she gave me
on the occasion of our parting
i figured out the fingering
and I played it better
than I had ever done
Tears came out of my eyes
because of the music
and the recollection
of her extraordinary beauty
which no one could avoid
and because she said
there was a missing song
and I had been employed

look down
look
down
that
lonesome
road

77

ALL HE KNOWS

All he knows
is that this has happened before—
this moment, next moment, last moment.
It is playing a second time,
maybe a third.
Yes, a third time.
He remembers remembering it.

Hydra,
August 1999

IF I TOOK A PILL

If I took a pill
I'd feel you so much better
I'd write you a poem
That sounds like a letter

I'd kill someone mean
And I'd cut off his ear
And I'd send it to you
With "I wish you were here"

I'm trying to finish
My shabby career
With a white cigarette
And a curtain of beer

I begged you to come
I begged on the phone
How wrong can you get
I was better alone

I am trying to finish
My shabby career
With a little truth
In the now and here

MOVING ON

I loved your face, I loved your hair
Your T-shirts and your eveningwear
As for the world, the job, the war
I ditched them all to love you more

And you're gone, now you're gone
As if there never was a you
Who broke the heart and made it new
Who's moving on, who's kidding who

I loved your moods, I loved the way
They threatened every single day
Your body ruled me, though it's true
'Twas more hormonal than the view

And now you're gone, now you're gone
As if there never was a you
Queen of lilac, Queen of blue
Who's moving on, who's kidding who

I loved your face, I loved your hair
Your T-shirts and your eveningwear
As for the world, the job, the war
I ditched them all to love you more

And now you're gone, now you're gone
As if there never was a you
Held me dying, pulled me through
Who's moving on, who's kidding who

if only
she hadn't

Saturday 1:40 am December 27, 2003

WAS I ALONE

Was I alone
   When we swore
      To keep it true

Was I alone
   Or was I there
      With you

Temptations
   There were more
      Than a few

Was I alone
   Or was I there
      With you

Was I alone
   When the mind
      Was split in two

Was I alone
   Or was I there
      With you

There was death
   But I knew
      What to do

Was I alone
   Or was I there
      With you

You'll have to wait
If you're waiting
For an argument
With me

You'll have to wait
Till it's over
And life and death
Agree

Somewhat
reluctant
to get
involved

January 13, 2004

COME AND SEE

come and see
they will say
you did not know me
they will say
you did not love me
they will say
you did not thirst
for the taste of me

they will say i lied
about our youthful encounter
when i lifted my hem
and i let my form shine through
the folds
of a terrible day

40 years i wandered
in your desert
a moment of your beauty
and 40 years of breathlessness
to balance it
40 years of remorse
40 years of disappointment

sleep which gives no rest
caress which does not calm
excitement with no background
arousal from no depth
the shallows of excitement
because it was not you

and a hand across my mouth
to silence me
a clever fatigue
to shut me down
a knot in my throat
a blow to the brain
a sweet distraction
to kill the appetite
a flush of sugar
to kill the appetite

and then forgetting you
for 40 years
building houses
for women
whom you sent
to remind me

see how i failed you
but that doesn't mean
it never happened

this began
and fizzled out
once again
too tired
to love you

or look for you
in the suffering

and did i forget to thank you
for what i felt
a moment ago
when you beckoned me
with god knows what
drunken promises

THANKS FOR THE DANCE

Thanks for the dance
It was hell, it was swell, it was fun
Thanks for all the dances
One two three, one two three one

There is a rose in your hair
Your shoulders are bare
It's a costume
But I'm a believer
So turn up the music
Pour out the wine
Stop at the surface
The surface is fine
We don't need to go any deeper

Thanks for the dance
I hear that we're married
One two three, one two three one
Thanks for the dance
And the baby you carried
It was almost a daughter or a son

And there's nothing to do
But to wonder if you
Are as tired as I am
Of leaving
We're joined in the spirit
Joined at the hip
Joined in the panic
Wondering if
We've come to some sort
Of agreement

Thanks for the dance
It was hell, it was swell, it was fun
Thanks for all the dances
One two three, one two three one

It was fine, it was fast
We were first, we were last
In line at the
Temple of Pleasure
But the green was so green
And the blue was so blue
I was so I
And you were so you
The crisis was light
As a feather

Thanks for the dance
It was hell, it was swell, it was fun
Thanks for all the
dances
One two three, one two three one

A STREET

I used to be your favourite drunk
Good for one more laugh
Then we both ran out of luck
And luck was all we had

You put on a uniform
To fight the Civil War
I tried to join but no one liked
The side I'm fighting for

So let's drink to when it's over
And let's drink to when we meet
I'll be standing on this corner
Where there used to be a street

You left me with the dishes
And a baby in the bath
And you're tight with the militias
You wear their camouflage

I guess that makes us equal
But I want to march with you
An extra in the sequel
To the old red-white-and-blue

So let's drink to when it's over
And let's drink to when we meet
I'll be standing on this corner
Where there used to be a street

I cried for you this morning
And I'll cry for you again
But I'm not in charge of sorrow
So please don't ask me when

I know the burden's heavy
As you bear it through the night
Some people say it's empty
But that doesn't mean it's light

So let's drink to when it's over
And let's drink to when we meet
I'll be standing on this corner
Where there used to be a street

It's going to be September now
For many years to come
Every heart adjusting
To the strict September drum

I see the Ghost of Culture
With the numbers on his wrist
Salute some new conclusion
Which all of us have missed

So let's drink to when it's over
And let's drink to when we meet
I'll be standing on this corner
Where there used to be a street

I PRAY FOR COURAGE

I pray for courage
Now I'm old
To greet the sickness
And the cold

I pray for courage
In the night
To bear the burden
Make it light

I pray for courage
In the time
When suffering comes and
Starts to climb

I pray for courage
At the end
To see death coming
As a friend

LYRICS

BLUE ALERT

BLUE ALERT

There's perfume burning in the air
Bits of beauty everywhere
Shrapnel flying; soldier hit the dirt
She comes so close. You feel her then
She tells you No and No again
Your lip is cut on the edge of her pleated skirt
Blue Alert

Visions of her drawing near
Arise, abide, and disappear
You try to slow it down; it doesn't work
It's just another night I guess
All tangled up in nakedness
You even touch yourself
You're such a flirt
Blue Alert

You know how nights like this begin
The kind of knot your heart gets in
Any way you turn is going to hurt
There's perfume burning in the air
Bits of beauty everywhere
Shrapnel flying; soldier hit the dirt
Blue Alert.

She breaks the rules so you can see
She's wilder than you'll ever be
You talk religion but she won't convert
Her body's twenty stories high
You try to look away, you try
But all you want to do is get there first
Blue Alert

The night I left
Bombay

Smelling the empty
bottle of Royal Musk

after a photo
taken by Bianca

INNERMOST DOOR

Nowhere to go
Nothing to say
You won't hear my voice
Till it's far, far away
I'm too tired now
To fight anymore
We're saying goodbye
At the innermost door

When I am alone
You'll come back to me
It's happened before
It's called memory

I must go back
To where we began
When I was a woman
And you were a man
If you come with me
I'll never begin
We made us a home
But the roof's fallen in

When I am alone
You'll come back to me
It's happened before
It's called memory

I'm not even sure
If I know where to start
But starting is second
First we must part
I'm too tired now
To fight anymore
We're saying goodbye
At the innermost door

THE GOLDEN GATE

Looking back, to San Francisco
Wearing my blue Chinese dress
A yellow jacket with padded shoulders
Smoking Sobranie cigarettes

Four o'clock and the fog comes in
We all remember the sea
For several seconds our sins are forgiven
Mine against you, yours against me

Don't wait for me and don't be sorry
Forget all the letters we wrote
Leave to the foghorns our lonesome story
Let them sustain the heavy note

We order another margarita
Sipping it slow by the window
Nobody needs an Indian teacher
All they need is San Francisco

For we are driving most carefully home
Down roads that are floating and veiled
The Golden Gate
It's still gold
It's still great
Nobody's drunk
Nothing has failed

HALF THE PERFECT WORLD

Every night she'd come to me
I'd cook for her, I'd pour her tea
She was in her thirties then
Had made some money, lived with men

We'd lay us down to give and get
Beneath the white mosquito net
And since no counting had begun
We lived a thousand years in one

The candles burned
The moon went down
The polished hill
The milky town
Transparent, weightless, luminous
Uncovering the two of us
On that fundamental ground
Where love's unwilled, unleashed,
Unbound
And half the perfect world is found

NIGHTINGALE

I built my house beside the wood
So I could hear you singing
And it was sweet and it was good
And love was all beginning

Fare thee well my nightingale
'Twas long ago I found you
Now all your songs of beauty fail
The forest gathers round you

The sun goes down behind a veil
'Tis now when you would call me
So rest in peace my nightingale
Beneath your branch of holly

Fare thee well my nightingale
I lived but to be near you
Though you are singing somewhere still
I can no longer hear you

NO ONE AFTER YOU

I danced with a lot of men
Fought in an ugly war
Gave my heart to a mountain
But I never loved before
I'm nervous when you turn away
My heart is always sore
Tuxedo gave me diamonds
But I never loved before

Been on the road forever
I'm always passing through
But you're my first love and my last
There is no one, no one after you

I've lived in many cities
From Paris to L.A.
I've known rags and riches
I'm a regular cliché
I tremble when you touch me
I want you more and more
I taught the Kama Sutra
But I never loved before

Been on the road forever
I'm always passing through
But you're my first love and my last
There is no one, no one after you

Thought I knew the facts of life
But now I know the score
Been around the block and back
But I never loved before

NEVER GOT TO LOVE YOU

The parking lot is empty
They killed the neon sign
It's dark from here to St. Jovite
It's dark all down the line
They ought to hand the night a ticket
For speeding: it's a crime
I had so much to tell you
But now it's closing time

I never got to love you
Like I heard it can be done
Where the differences are many
But the heart is always one

The memories come back empty
Like their batteries are low
It feels like you just left me
Tho' it happened years ago
They're stacking up the chairs
Wiping down the bar
I never got to tell you
How beautiful you are

I never got to love you
Like I heard it can be done
Where the differences are many
But the heart is always one

Don't know how it happened
But I missed the exit sign
It's dark from here to St. Jovite
It's dark all down the line

THE MIST

As the mist leaves no scar
On the dark green hill
So my body leaves no scar
On you, nor ever will

When wind and hawk encounter
What remains to keep?
So you and I encounter
Then turn then fall to sleep

As many nights endure
Without a moon or star
So will we endure
When one is gone and far

CRAZY TO LOVE YOU

I had to go crazy to love you
Had to go down to the pit
Had to do time in the tower
Now I'm too tired to quit

I had to go crazy to love you
You who were never the one
Whom I chased through the souvenir heartache
My braids and my blouse all undone

Sometimes I'd head for the highway
I'm old and the mirrors don't lie
But crazy has places to hide me
Deeper than saying goodbye

I had to go crazy to love you
Had to let everything fall
Had to be people I hated
Had to be no one at all

Tired of choosing desire
I've been saved by a blessed fatigue
The gates of commitment unwired
And nobody trying to leave

Sometimes I'd head for the highway
I'm old and the mirrors don't lie
But crazy has places to hide me
Deeper than saying goodbye

THANKS FOR THE DANCE

Thanks for the dance
I'm sorry you're tired
The evening has hardly begun
Thanks for the dance
Try to look inspired
One two three, one two three one

There's a rose in my hair
My shoulders are bare
I've been wearing this
        costume forever
Turn up the music
Pour out the wine
Stop at the surface
The surface is fine
We don't need to go any deeper

Thanks for the dance
I hear that we're married
One two three, one two three one
Thanks for the dance
And the baby I carried
It was almost a daughter or a son

And there's nothing to do
But to wonder if you
Are as hopeless as me
And as decent
We're joined in the spirit
Joined at the hip
Joined in the panic
Wondering if
We've come to some sort
Of agreement

It was fine it was fast
I was first I was last
In line at the Temple of Pleasure
But the green was so green
And the blue was so blue
I was so I
And you were so you
The crisis was light
As a feather

Thanks for the dance
It's been hell, it's been swell,
It's been fun
Thanks for all the dances
One two three, one two three one

OLD IDEAS

GOING HOME

I love to speak with Leonard
He's a sportsman and a shepherd
He's a lazy bastard living in a suit,
Living in a suit

But he does say what I tell him
Even though it isn't welcome
He just doesn't have the freedom
To refuse

He will speak these words of wisdom
Like a sage, a man of vision
Though he knows he's really nothing
But the brief elaboration of a tube
Going home
Without my sorrow
Going home
Sometime tomorrow
Going home
To where it's better
Than before
Going home
Without my burden
Going home
Behind the curtain

Going home
Without the costume
That I wore

He wants to write a love song
An anthem of forgiving
A manual for living with defeat
A cry above the suffering
A sacrifice recovering
But that isn't what I need him to complete

I want to make him certain
That he doesn't have a burden
That he doesn't need a vision
That he only has permission
To do my instant bidding
Which is to SAY what I have told him
To repeat

Going home
Without my sorrow
Going home
Sometime tomorrow
Going home
To where it's better
Than before

Going home
Without my burden
Going home
Behind the curtain
Going home
Without this costume
That I wore

I love to speak with Leonard
He's a sportsman and a shepherd
He's a lazy bastard
Living in a suit

AMEN

Tell me again
When I've been to the river
And I've taken the edge off my thirst
Tell me again
We're alone & I'm listening
I'm listening so hard that it hurts

Tell me again
When I'm clean and I'm sober
Tell me again
When I've seen through the horror
Tell me again
Tell me over and over
Tell me you want me then
Amen

Tell me again
When the victims are singing
And Laws of Remorse are restored
Tell me again
That you know what I'm thinking
But vengeance belongs to the lord

listening
&
carefully

Tell me again
When I'm clean and I'm sober
Tell me again
When I've seen through the horror
Tell me again
Tell me over and over
Tell me that you love me then
Amen
Amen
Amen
Amen

Tell me again
When the day has been ransomed
& night has no right to begin
Try me again
When the angels are panting
And scratching the door to come in

Tell me again
When I'm clean and I'm sober
Tell me again
When I've seen through the horror
Tell me again
Tell me over and over
Tell me that you need me then
Amen
Amen
Amen
Amen

Tell me again
When the filth of the butcher
Is washed in the blood of the lamb
Tell me again
When the rest of the culture
Has passed thru' the
Eye of the Camp

Tell me again
When I'm clean and I'm sober
Tell me again
When I've seen through the horror
Tell me again
Tell me over and over
Tell me that you love me then
Amen
Amen
Amen
Amen

SHOW ME THE PLACE

Show me the place
Where you want your slave to go
Show me the place
I've forgotten, I don't know
Show me the place
For my head is bending low
Show me the place
Where you want your slave to go

Show me the place
Help me roll away the stone
Show me the place
I can't move this thing alone
Show me the place
Where the Word became a man
Show me the place
Where the suffering began

The troubles came
I saved what I could save
A thread of light
A particle a wave
But there were chains
So I hastened to behave
There were chains
So I loved you like a slave

Show me the place
Where you want your slave to go
Show me the place
I've forgotten, I don't know

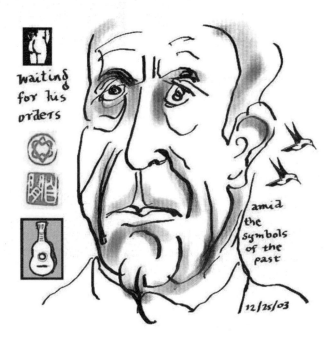

waiting
for his
orders

amid
the
symbols
of the
past

12/25/03

DARKNESS

I caught the darkness
Drinking from your cup
I caught the darkness
Drinking from your cup
I said: Is this contagious?
You said: Just drink it up

I got no future
I know my days are few
The present's not that pleasant
Just a lot of things to do
I thought the past would last me
But the darkness got that too

I should have seen it coming
It was right behind your eyes
You were young and it was summer
I just had to take a dive
Winning you was easy
But darkness was the prize

I don't smoke no cigarette
I don't drink no alcohol
I ain't had much loving yet
But that's always been your call
Hey I don't miss it baby
I got no taste for anything at all

I used to love the rainbow
I used to love the view
I loved the early morning
I'd pretend that it was new
But I caught the darkness baby
And I got it worse than you

113

I caught the darkness
Drinking from your cup
I caught the darkness
Drinking from your cup
I said: Is this contagious?
You said: Just drink it up

ANYHOW

It's a shame and it's a pity
The way you treat me now
I know you can't forgive me
But forgive me anyhow

The ending got so ugly
Even heard you say
You never ever loved me
Oh but love me anyway

Dreamed about you baby
You were wearing half your dress
I know you have to hate me
But could you hate me less?

I used up all my chances
And you'll never take me back
But there ain't no harm in asking
Could you cut me one more slack?

I'm naked and I'm filthy
And there's sweat upon my brow
And both of us are guilty
Anyhow

Have mercy on me baby
After all I did confess
Even though you have to hate me
Could you hate me less?

It's a shame and it's a pity
I know you can't forgive me
The ending got so ugly
You never ever loved me

Dreamed about you baby
I know you have to hate me
I'm naked and I'm filthy
And both of us are guilty
Anyhow

Have mercy on me baby

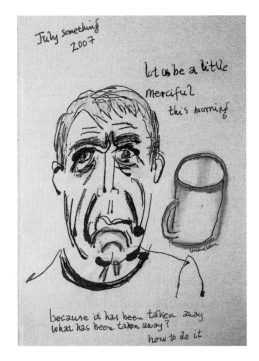

114

CRAZY TO LOVE YOU

Had to go crazy to love you
Had to go down to the pit
Had to do time in the tower
Begging my crazy to quit

Had to go crazy to love you
You who were never the one
Whom I chased through the souvenir heartache
Her braids and her blouse all undone

Sometimes I'd head for the highway
I'm old and the mirrors don't lie
But crazy has places to hide in
Deeper than saying goodbye

Had to go crazy to love you
Had to let everything fall
Had to be people I hated
Had to be no one at all

I'm tired of choosing desire
Been saved by a sweet fatigue
The gates of commitment unwired
And nobody trying to leave

the mirror in my room
after a photo taken by the
great painter of mood Bianca
Nixdorf Kemps Corner Hotel
2003

Sometimes I'd head for the highway
I'm old and the mirrors don't lie
But crazy has places to hide in
Deeper than saying goodbye

Had to go crazy to love you
You who were never the one
Whom I chased through the souvenir heartache
Her braids and her blouse all undone

COME HEALING

O gather up the brokenness
And bring it to me now
The fragrance of those
promises
You never dared to vow

The splinters that you carry
The cross you left behind
Come healing of the body
Come healing of the mind

And let the heavens hear it
The penitential hymn
Come healing of the spirit
Come healing of the limb

Behold the gates of mercy
In arbitrary space
And none of us deserving
The cruelty or the grace

O solitude of longing
Where love has been confined
Come healing of the body
Come healing of the mind

O see the darkness yielding
That tore the light apart
Come healing of the reason
Come healing of the heart

O troubled dust concealing
An undivided love
The Heart beneath is teaching
To the broken Heart above

116

O let the heavens falter
And let the earth proclaim:
Come healing of the Altar
Come healing of the Name

O longing of the branches
To lift the little bud
O longing of the arteries
To purify the blood

And let the heavens hear it
The penitential hymn
Come healing of the spirit
Come healing of the limb

O let the heavens hear it
The penitential hymn
Come healing of the spirit
Come healing of the limb

BANJO

There's something that I'm watching
Means a lot to me
It's a broken banjo bobbing
On the dark infested sea

Don't know how it got there
Maybe taken by the wave
Off of someone's shoulder
Or out of someone's grave

It's coming for me darling
No matter where I go
Its duty is to harm me
My duty is to know

There's something that I'm watching
Means a lot to me
It's a broken banjo bobbing
On the dark infested sea

LULLABY

Sleep baby sleep
The day's on the run
The wind in the trees
Is talking in tongues

If your heart is torn
I don't wonder why
If the night is long
Here's my lullaby

Well the mouse ate the crumb
Then the cat ate the crust
Now they've fallen in love
They're talking in tongues

If your heart is torn
I don't wonder why
If the night is long
Here's my lullaby

Sleep baby sleep
There's a morning to come
The wind in the trees
they're talking in tongues

If your heart is torn
I don't wonder why
If the night is long
Here's my lullaby

119

DIFFERENT SIDES

We find ourselves on different sides
Of a line that nobody drew
Though it all may be one in the higher eye
Down here where we live it is two

I to my side call the meek and the mild
You to your side call the Word
By virtue of suffering I claim to have won
You claim to have never been heard

Both of us say there are laws to obey
But frankly I don't like your tone
You want to change the way I make love
I want to leave it alone

The pull of the moon the thrust of the sun
And thus the ocean is crossed
The waters are blessed while a shadowy guest
Kindles a light for the lost

Both of us say there are laws to obey
But frankly I don't like your tone
You want to change the way I make love
I want to leave it alone

Down in the valley the famine goes on
The famine up on the hill
I say that you shouldn't you couldn't you can't
You say that you must and you will

Both of us say there are laws to obey
But frankly I don't like your tone
You want to change the way I make love
I want to leave it alone

You want to live where the suffering is
I want to get out of town
C'mon baby give me a kiss
Stop writing everything down

Both of us say there are laws to obey
But frankly I don't like your tone
You want to change the way I make love
I want to leave it alone

Both of us say there are laws to obey
But frankly I don't like your tone
You want to change the way I make love
I want to leave it alone

POPULAR PROBLEMS

SLOW

I'm slowing down the tune
I never liked it fast
You want to get there soon
I want to get there last

It's not because I'm old
It's not the life I led
I always liked it slow
That's what my momma said

I'm lacing up my shoe
But I don't want to run
I'll get here when I do
Don't need no starting gun

It's not because I'm old
It's not what dying does
I always liked it slow
Slow is in my blood

I always liked it slow:
I never liked it fast
With you it's got to go:
With me it's got to last

It's not because I'm old
It's not because I'm dead
I always liked it slow
That's what my momma said

All your moves are swift
All your turns are tight
Let me catch my breath
I thought we had all night

I like to take my time
I like to linger as it flies
A weekend on your lips
A lifetime in your eyes

I always liked it slow:
I never liked it fast
With you it's got to go:
With me it's got to last

It's not because I'm old
It's not the life I led
I always liked it slow
That's what my momma said

I'm slowing down the tune
I never liked it fast
You want to get there soon
I want to get there last

So baby let me go
You're wanted back in town
In case they want to know
I'm just trying to slow it down

4/5/03

getting
there
at last

ALMOST LIKE THE BLUES

I saw some people starving
There was murder, there was rape
Their villages were burning
They were trying to escape
I couldn't meet their glances
I was staring at my shoes
It was acid, it was tragic
It was almost like the blues

I have to die a little
Between each murderous thought
And when I'm finished thinking
I have to die a lot
There's torture and there's killing
There's all my bad reviews
The war, the children missing
Lord, it's almost like the blues

I let my heart get frozen
To keep away the rot
My father says I'm chosen
My mother says I'm not
I listened to their story
Of the Gypsies and the Jews
It was good, it wasn't boring
It was almost like the blues

There is no G-d in Heaven
And there is no Hell below
So says the great professor
Of all there is to know
But I've had the invitation
That a sinner can't refuse
And it's almost like salvation
It's almost like the blues

SAMSON IN NEW ORLEANS

You said that you were with me
You said you were my friend
Did you really love the city
Or did you just pretend

You said you loved her secrets
And her freedoms hid away
She was better than America
That's what I heard you say

You said how could this happen
You said how can this be
The remnant all dishonored
On the bridge of misery

And we who cried for mercy
From the bottom of the pit
Was our prayer so
    damn unworthy
The Son rejected it?

So gather up the killers
Get everyone in town
Stand me by those pillars
Let me take this
    temple down

The king so kind and solemn
He wears a bloody crown
So stand me by that column
Let me take this temple down

You said how could this happen
You said how can this be
The chains are gone from heaven
The storms are wild and free

There's other ways to answer
That certainly is true
Me, I'm blind with death
    and anger
And that's no place for you

There's a woman
    in the window
And a bed in Tinsel Town
I'll write you when it's over
Let me take this
    temple down

October 14, 2007
Sunday 7:30 am

no longer inclined
to speak the truth

speak truth to power?
        rather
speak truth
    to the powerless

A STREET

I used to be your favorite drunk
Good for one more laugh
Then we both ran out of luck
Luck was all we ever had

You put on a uniform
To fight the Civil War
You looked so good I didn't care
What side you're fighting for

It wasn't all that easy
When you up and walked away
But I'll save that little story
For another rainy day

I know the burden's heavy
As you wheel it through the night
Some people say it's empty
But that don't mean it's light

You left me with the dishes
And a baby in the bath
You're tight with the militias
You wear their camouflage

You always said we're equal
So let me march with you
Just an extra in the sequel
To the old red white and blue

Baby don't ignore me
We were smokers we were friends
Forget that tired story
Of betrayal and revenge

I see the Ghost of Culture
With numbers on his wrist
Salute some new conclusion
Which all of us have missed

I cried for you this morning
And I'll cry for you again
But I'm not in charge of sorrow
So please don't ask me when

There may be wine and roses

DID I EVER LOVE YOU

Did I ever love you
Did I ever need you
Did I ever fight you
Did I ever want to

Did I ever leave you
Was I ever able
Are we still leaning
Across the old table

Did I ever love you
Did I ever need you
Did I ever fight you
Did I ever want to

Did I ever leave you
Was I ever able
Are we still leaning
Across the old table

Was it ever settled
Was it ever over
And is it still raining
Back in November

The lemon trees blossom
The almond trees wither
Was I ever someone
Who could love you forever

Was it ever settled
Was it ever over
And is it still raining
Back in November

The lemon trees blossom
The almond trees wither
It's Spring and it's Summer
And it's Winter forever

Did I ever love you
Does it really matter
Did I ever fight you
You don't need to answer

Did I ever leave you
Was I ever able
Are we still leaning
Across the old table

Did I ever love you
Did I ever need you
Did I ever fight you
Did I ever want to

Did I ever leave you
Was I ever able
Are we still leaning
Across the old table

MY OH MY

Wasn't hard to love you
Didn't have to try
Wasn't hard to love you
Didn't have to try
Held you for a little while
My Oh My Oh My

Drove you to the station
Never asked you why
Drove you to the station
Never asked you why
Held you for a little while
My Oh My Oh My

All the boys are waving
Trying to catch your eye
All the boys are waving
Trying to catch your eye
Held you for a little while
My Oh My Oh My

Wasn't hard to love you
Didn't have to try
Wasn't hard to love you
Didn't have to try
Held you for a little while
My Oh My Oh My

NEVER MIND

The war was lost
The treaty signed
I was not caught
I crossed the line

I was not caught
Though many tried
I live among you
Well disguised

I had to leave
My life behind
I dug some graves
You'll never find

The story's told
With facts and lies
I had a name
But never mind

Never mind
Never mind
The war was lost
The treaty signed

There's truth that lives
And truth that dies
I don't know which
So never mind

Your victory
Was so complete
That some among you
Thought to keep

A record of
Our little lives
The clothes we wore
Our spoons our knives

a dreadful night
visited by the dear ghosts
of my favourite lovers
all of them
at their most skillful
and insistent persuasions

135

The games of luck
Our soldiers played
The stones we cut
The songs we made

Our law of peace
Which understands
A husband leads
A wife commands

And all of this
Expressions of
The Sweet Indifference
Some call Love

The High Indifference
Some call Fate
But we had Names
More intimate

Names so deep
and Names so true
They're blood to me
They're dust to you

There is no need
That this survive
There's truth that lives
And truth that dies

Never mind
Never mind
I live the life
I left behind

There's truth that lives
And truth that dies
I don't know which
So never mind

I could not kill
The way you kill
I could not hate
I tried I failed

You turned me in
At least you tried
You side with them
Whom you despise

This was your heart
This swarm of flies
This was once your mouth
This bowl of lies

You serve them well
I'm not surprised
You're of their kin
You're of their kind

Never mind
Never mind
The story's told
With facts and lies
You own the world
So never mind

Never mind
Never mind
I live the life
I left behind

I live it full
I live it wide
Through layers of time
You can't divide

My woman's here
My children too
Their graves are safe
From ghosts like you

In places deep
With roots entwined
I live the life
I left behind

BORN IN CHAINS

I was born in chains
But I was taken out of Egypt
I was bound to a burden
But the burden it was raised
Lord I can no longer
Keep this secret
Blessed is the Name
The Name be praised

I fled to the edge
Of the Mighty Sea of Sorrow
Pursued by the riders
Of a cruel and dark regime
But the waters parted
And my soul crossed over
Out of Egypt
Out of Pharaoh's dream

Word of Words
And Measure of all Measures
Blessed is the Name
The Name be blessed
Written on my heart
In burning Letters
That's all I know
I cannot read the rest

I was idle with my soul
When I heard that you could use me
I followed very closely
My life remained the same
But then you showed me
Where you had been wounded
In every atom
Broken is the Name

I was alone on the road
Your Love was so confusing
And all my teachers told me

That I had myself to blame
But in the Grip
Of Sensual Illusion
A sweet unknowing
Unified the Name

Word of Words
And Measure of all Measures
Blessed is the Name
The Name be blessed
Written on my heart
In burning Letters
That's all I know
I cannot read the rest

I've heard the soul unfolds
In the chambers of its longing
And the bitter liquor sweetens
In the hammered cup
But all the Ladders
Of the Night have fallen
Only darkness now
To lift the Longing up

YOU GOT ME SINGING

You got me singing
Even tho' the news is bad
You got me singing
The only song I ever had
You got me singing
Ever since the river died
You got me thinking
Of the places we could hide
You got me singing
Even though the world is gone
You got me thinking
I'd like to carry on
You got me singing
Even tho' it all looks grim
You got me singing
The Hallelujah hymn
You got me singing
Like a prisoner in a jail
You got me singing
Like my pardon's in the mail
You got me wishing
Our little love would last
You got me thinking
Like those people of the past

YOU WANT IT DARKER

YOU WANT IT DARKER

If you are the dealer
I'm out of the game
If you are the healer
I'm broken and lame
If thine is the glory
Then mine must be the shame
You want it darker
We kill the flame

Magnified and sanctified
Be Thy Holy Name
Vilified and crucified
In the human frame
A million candles burning
For the help that never came
You want it darker
We kill the flame

Hineni Hineni
I'm ready, my Lord

There's a lover in the story
But the story is still the same
There's a lullaby for suffering
And a paradox to blame
But it's written in the scriptures
And it's not some idle claim
You want it darker
We kill the flame

They're lining up the prisoners
The guards are taking aim
I struggled with some demons
They were middle-class and tame
Didn't know I had permission
To murder and to maim
You want it darker

Hineni Hineni
I'm ready, my Lord

Magnified and sanctified
Be Thy Holy Name
Vilified and crucified
In the human frame
A million candles burning
For the love that never came
You want it darker
We kill the flame

If you are the dealer
I'm out of the game
If you are the healer
I'm broken and lame
If thine is the glory
Then mine must be the shame
You want it darker
We kill the flame

Hineni Hineni
I'm ready, my Lord

everything will
Come back
in the wrong light
completely
    misunderstood
and I will be seen
as the man
I devoted much of
    my life
to not being

2/4/03

TREATY

I seen you change the water into wine
I seen you change it back to water too
I sit at your table every night
I try but I just don't get high with you

I wish there was a treaty we could sign
I do not care who takes this bloody hill
I'm angry and I'm tired all the time
I wish there was a treaty
I wish there was a treaty
Between your love and mine

They're dancing in the street—it's Jubilee
We sold ourselves for love but now we're free
I'm so sorry for the ghost I made you be
Only one of us was real—and that was me.

I haven't said a word since you've been gone
That any liar couldn't say as well
I just can't believe the static coming on
You were my ground—my safe and sound
You were my aerial

The fields are crying out—it's Jubilee
We sold ourselves for love but now we're free
I'm so sorry for the ghost I made you be
Only one of us was real—and that was me.

I heard the snake was baffled by his sin
He shed his scales to find the snake within
But born again is born without a skin
The poison enters into everything

I wish there was a treaty we could sign
I do not care who takes the bloody hill
I'm angry and I'm tired all the time
I wish there was a treaty
I wish there was a treaty
Between your love and mine

I wish there was a treaty we could sign
It's over now, the water and the wine
We were broken then, but now we're borderline
I wish there was a treaty
I wish there was a treaty
Between your love and mine

ON THE LEVEL

I knew that it was wrong
I didn't have a doubt
I was dying to get back home
And you were starting out

I said I best be moving on
You said, we have all day
You smiled at me like I was young
It took my breath away

Your crazy fragrance all around
Your secrets all in view
My lost, my lost was saying found
My don't was saying do

Let's keep it on the level
When I walked away from you
I turned my back on the devil
Turned my back on the angel too

They ought to give my heart a medal
For letting go of you
When I turned my back on the devil
Turned my back on the angel too

Now I'm living in this temple
Where they tell you what to do
I'm old and I've had to settle
On a different point of view

I was fighting with temptation
But I didn't want to win
A man like me don't like to see
Temptation caving in

Your crazy fragrance all around
Your secrets in my view
My lost, my lost was saying found
My don't was saying do

Let's keep it on the level
When I walked away from you
I turned my back on the devil
Turned my back on the angel too

They ought to give my heart a medal
For letting go of you
When I turned my back on the devil
Turned my back on the angel too

the temptation
of the halos
resisted

LEAVING THE TABLE

I'm leaving the table
I'm out of the game
I don't know the people
In your picture frame
If I ever loved you
It's a crying shame
If I ever loved you
If I knew your name

You don't need a lawyer
I'm not making a claim
You don't need to surrender
I'm not taking aim
I don't need a lover
The wretched beast is tame
I don't need a lover
So blow out the flame

There's nobody missing
There is no reward
Little by little
We're cutting the cord
We're spending the treasure
That love cannot afford
I know you can feel it
The sweetness restored

I don't need a reason
For what I became
I've got these excuses
They're tired and lame
I don't need a pardon
There's no one left to blame
I'm leaving the table
I'm out of the game

IF I DIDN'T HAVE YOUR LOVE

If the sun would lose its light
And we lived an endless night
And there was nothing left
That you could feel
That's how it would be
What the world would seem to me
If I didn't have your love
To make it real

If the stars were all unpinned
And a cold and bitter wind
Swallowed up the world
Without a trace
Well that's where I would be
What my life would seem to me
If I couldn't lift the veil
And see your face

If no leaves were on the tree
And no water in the sea
And the break of day
Had nothing to reveal
That's how broken I would be
What my life would seem to me
If I didn't have your love
To make it real

If the sun would lose its light
And we lived an endless night
And there was nothing left
That you could feel
If the sea were sand alone
And the flowers made of stone
And no one that you hurt
Could ever heal
That's how broken I would be
What my life would seem to me
If I didn't have your love
To make it real

TRAVELING LIGHT

I'm traveling light
It's au revoir
My once so bright
My fallen star

I'm running late
They'll close the bar
I used to play
One mean guitar

I guess I'm just
Somebody who
Has given up
On the me and you
I'm not alone
I've met a few
Traveling light like
We used to do

Goodnight goodnight
My fallen star
I guess you're right
You always are

I know you're right
About the blues
You live some life
You'd never choose

I'm just a fool
A dreamer who
Forgot to dream
Of the me and you
I am not alone
I've met a few
Traveling light like
We used to do

this is
the the
end of
it!

Traveling light
It's au revoir
My once so bright
My fallen star

I'm running late
They'll close the bar
I used to play
One mean guitar

I guess I'm just
Somebody who
Has given up
On the me and you
I'm not alone
I've met a few
Traveling light like
We used to do

But if the road
Leads back to you
Must I forget
The things I knew
When I was friends
With one or two
Traveling light like
We used to do
I'm traveling light

IT SEEMED THE BETTER WAY

It seemed the better way
When first I heard him speak
But now it's much too late
To turn the other cheek

Sounded like the truth
Seemed the better way
Sounded like the truth
But it's not the truth today

I wonder what it was
I wonder what it meant
At first he touched on love
But then he touched on death

I better hold my tongue
I better take my place
Lift this glass of blood
Try to say the grace

hopeless
trees

STEER YOUR WAY

Steer your way through the ruins of the Altar and the Mall
Steer your way through the fables of Creation and The Fall
Steer your way past the Palaces that rise above the rot
Year by year
Month by month
Day by day
Thought by thought

Steer your heart past the Truth you believed in yesterday
Such as Fundamental Goodness and the Wisdom of the Way
Steer your heart, precious heart, past the women whom you bought
Year by year
Month by month
Day by day
Thought by thought

Steer your way through the pain that is far more real than you
That has smashed the Cosmic Model that has blinded every View
And please don't make me go there, tho' there be a God or not
Year by year
Month by month
Day by day
Thought by thought

They whisper still, the injured stones, the blunted mountains weep
As he died to make men holy, let us die to make things cheap
And say the Mea Culpa, which you've probably forgot
Year by year
Month by month
Day by day
Thought by thought

Steer your way, O my heart, tho' I have no right to ask,
To the one who was never, never equal to the task
Who knows he's been convicted, who knows he will be shot
Year by year
Month by month
Day by day
Thought by thought

LEONARD AND PETER

Peter Dale Scott (b. 1929), a poet and scholar, is Professor Emeritus at the University of California, Berkeley. He is the son of Canadian poet F. R. Scott, who was Cohen's tutor at McGill University. Scott sent Cohen an inscribed copy of his most recent volume of poems, *Walking on Darkness*. The subsequent e-mail exchange is recorded here, courtesy of Scott. The final text message is courtesy of Rebecca De Mornay.

Leonard (from "You Want It Darker," September 21, 2016):

You want it darker / We kill the flame. . . .

Peter (inscription in *Walking on Darkness*, October 1, 2016):

If *you want it darker*
This book is not for you
I have always wanted it lighter
And I think God does too

Leonard (October 3, 2016):

who says "i" want it darker?
who says the "you" is "me"?
god saved you in your harbor
while millions died at sea

you and god are buddies
you know his wishes now
here's broken Job all bloodied
who met him brow to brow

there is a voice so powerful
so easily unheard
those that hear may hate it all
but follow every word

if you have not been asked
to squat above the dead
be happy that you're deaf
not something worse instead

he will make it darker
he will make it light
according to his torah
which leonard did not write

159

Peter (October 4, 2016):

Who says I know God's wishes?
I've not met brow to brow
never had a chance to glimpse him
and never hope to now

But we who were raised in harbors
while others burned from war
have been free to choose which voices
made us what we are.

Leonard (October 4, 2016):

That was great fun.
Be well, dear friends.
Much love,
Eliezer

Leonard (November 6, 2016, 3 p.m., in response to a photo of Peter and Sophia De Mornay-O'Neal):

Blessed are the peacemakers: for they shall be called the children of God.

Selections from THE NOTEBOOKS

but the times are long

it's all a long time gone
when I had an honest job
and Annie called me darling

***

I don't want to greet
the morning light
with a night like this
    in my heart soul
Have mercy on those shadows
that fall in love with shadows

***

You're going to fall some day
into a wild embrace
with one who turns away
so you cannot see his face

You won't know who you are
You won't know who he is
There's no one there to know
a love so wild as this

He won't be there before you
He won't be here within
There'll be no border to the heart
or boundary to the skin

He isn't there before you
isn't here within
No border to the heart
or boundary to the skin

***

When we are apart
and the moon is full

My longing
paints your hands
on the full moon

If you read this by candlelight
as it was written
if you are alone in a room
as I am
you will know that I love you
dear and distant wife

***

Formless dinosaurs

Ignorant of our stern judgement
the dinosaurs graze on stars
in the fields of night
I have no sorrow left

I neglected you a long time
but I neglected myself even longer

This night will never end
The morning will come to wash it away
with sunlight and commotion

I have no sorrow left
The stars are too dim for the night

I have no sorrow left
for the dinosaur
grazing on stars
in the fields of night

***

I loved my friends
I talked to them
for hours and hours

and I began
to want to be beautiful
and I grew
to hate beauty in others

Mind you
a monster
is not always beautiful

***

and here is a voice
I have been listening to
for a long time
it says: O G-d, I love you
it says: Child, I love you back

***

Wednesday 17th May 00

Thanks for turning me on
with your hatred of sex and men
and your drunken kisses
which were like someone
trying to eat my voice raw
like a living oyster

The Tibetan fairy-tales
of coming back
in a brand-new sack
to finish off your dinner

right to the end I wanted you
right to the bitter end
your breath like a morgue
your flesh undone
your juices gone
I was still sifting through
your boring conversation
for traces, for hints
that you ever thought of me

with longing
and found none

Thank you Heather
thanks for turning me on

and after a while I gave up
trying to satisfy you
I just wanted to stick it in
under any circumstances

self-respect, tenderness
every mask was torn
just a hunger with an arm
thanks for turning me on
just to be inside of you
just to know
for one fraction of a measure
that we were in
the world together
thank you, Beloved
for turning me off
and for turning me on

I thank the nameless one
and I thank the nameless many

***

L.A.
Friday August 5[?], 2000

I wanted you to love me
I needed you to love me
I had to have you love me
but what I meant
or who I meant
I still don't have a clue
except that I was lonely
and there was only you

***

9 am   Sunday, Aug 7, 2000

If they never played the game
how could they know the score
Don't go down to Westmount Station
Those trains don't run no more

The bullet trains of Tokyo
The monorail
The TGV
They'll let you know
   what transportation's for
But don't go down to Westm't Station
Those old trains don't run no more

Those stories that your father knows

***

Friday August 11 [?]

I came to you with sorrow .
and I promised more tomorrow
you said, Come to Me with bread
I said, Lord, I am a victim
I cannot make a living
That's why you employed me with the dead

***

she loved me
   I'm only quoting her
she's gone now
   I feel much quieter
no beauty
   but then neither am I
alone now

***

he wasn't as lean as Bogart
or short as Alan Ladd
but his songs would last forever
and some already had

167

I could have been the Ace of Spades
if I was only black
I could have been the Prince of Peace
but Jesus's coming back
I could have been the Beauty Queen
but I had too much hair
I could have stood where Moses stood
but he was standing there
I could have been a millionaire
but money ruined my life
I could have been the Master [?]
I didn't want your wife

As a child I had the dream
that I might speak in the highest name
and gather many broken {noble} hearts
to homeward [?]
and I was judged by those
who spoke more sweetly than I could
and I was judged by those
whose suffering made them dumb
The judgement was, Be silent, child
be silent in the world of men
O bitter silence that I held
while omens burned the gypsy [?] dust
and wires cut the {faithful} {widow?} riders down
and every holy word was turned
to serve the greed and muting of mind
O bitter silence, bitter calm I spread
while every soul {law} was drowned
below the poison tide and now the vile
abominations rose to rule and regulate
the very breathing of the soul
and still the judgement was
Be silent, Child, you are too weak {you are too rich},
you are too young

and this world came, and men like you and me, gold in the tooth, gold in the
taste, gold in the brain, and great champions of silence came, missionaries of
the void, and someone said, and someone said there's nothing left, there's
nothing next, be human in the human world, be calm, be calm, and in my
heart I hated this vast tyranny of peace. I could not hear the judgement and I
fell in love with everyone who fell in love with me

***

Simple Songs
    with everybody singing
and someone saying
    sing us "Born to Lose"
and Hershorn takes
    his daughter's ukulele
and everybody listens
    to the news

Simple songs with everybody singing
I forget them soon I let them go
The anthems & the prayers of lonely people

***

It is going to be like this
Sitting at a bar in Geneva
or is it Zurich
I can never tell which
Carolina, Carolina
I can never tell which

Bridge
    It is a nice place here
    They don't mind you smoking either

Everybody's smoking & drinking
in Geneva or Zurich
Carolina, Carolina
are we ever
    going to get together again
Sometimes I think so
    Sometimes I don't
I don't think I do tonight
    I think I don't
Carolina, Carolina,
    in Zurich or Geneva

I don't think we're going
to get together ever again

***

169

This time, baby, gonna ask for the moon
gonna ask the rainbow to deliver
the treasure right now, not later, not soon
If it rains, the rain's got to be silver
got to hear it in the arms of my lover
no other place will do. I want it all,
the whole fucking cross, not just a splinter.
I don't just want my kick, I want the ball
and if it's got to be a stone, I want the wall.

Take my gloves
Take my helmet
take my belt
my forty-five
I don't need them
where I'm going

you don't have to talk no more
you can rest awhile
There ain't no words
           where you are going

O my fathers
I have listened
to your whispering
in the air
I have heard you
talk all morning
Midnight I have
heard your prayer

Take my knife
my silver bullets
take the woman
by my side
I can't have her,
where I'm going
I can't even
tell her why

***

all those broken hearts
& you ain't gonna stop it
when it starts

***

Baby, I can't speak {talk} about
the hundred thousand darknesses
that go around insisting
they're my heart
I can talk about the weather
I don't think it's going to rain
but if you ask me how I am:
I can't complain

You can say
    it's all been written
but I cannot read the text
It's love alone distracts me
from one moment to the next

I'd never seen the day so new
the green so green, the blue so blue
and all you lost was
only to renew you

I tried to make a joyful now

Surely the ocean will part her lips
for the widow watching

Surely the nighttime
    will yield another song
Surely the ocean
    will let the men undrown
Surely the widow
    will give another chance
to the widow who's been
    watching all the ships

Surely the morning light
    will let the man return
and the wolf go back
                    to moonlight
Surely the moonlight
    will hold another face

The heart of love is covered up
        & the heart of labour too
There's no one else
            There's nothing else
can move the dust but you

all the bad examples of my uncles
and my friends
still I could not fight it
or wrong or even right it
I didn't even know
what I'd done

Now Bobby left his body
    in a Hong Kong Hotel
He never even told us where
    to find it

I was looking for the needle
I was looking high & low
for the needle that I used to sew
my coat of many colours long ago
that I lost so long ago

I've been waiting
    many years now
for a climate
    such as this
for the cold to
    be so clear now
that nobody even
    talks about the spring

Here comes the morning boat
here comes the evening train
here comes Marianne now
to say goodbye again

***

Athens   Inter, C.   July 30

a dream a couple of nights ago
a fierce god came thru the door
almost broke down the door
my house was a frail affair

***

Sept 17, 2008

you who have fallen
beneath all contempt
whose {your} pockets are {full swollen}
but you're living in debt

and dead to the culture
that murdered your {heart} pride
you pick through the scriptures
for somewhere to hide

***

Oct 16

There was so little to say
All my prophecies
were coming true
I was old
My work was done
Then you began
to undress for me
on Skype
And I had to think
about my life again

It was a good hotel
Thick double curtain
sealed the room in darkness
any time of the day
I lay on my {the} bed
in my free time
thinking of her {you}
as if {I was} meditating

***

Geneva dressing rm.   Oct 26 2008

a few nights ago
in a dream
you said: "Come along
to the sunny beach"
I thought you meant
"just you and me"
but it turned out
you were with a handsome young man

named Coran
and I was, as you said,
welcome to "come along"

and that was that

***

Dream Brighton   Nov 28[?]

Tom Waits singing—I hear him
I'm in a theatre—I've given
a show to a large audience
My show went well—I can't
see him—I'm in my dressing
room—but I can hear him—
his music begin—it is so
beautiful and original and
sophisticated—so much better
than mine—some mélange

of harshness and sweetness—
modern and sentimental all
at once—even Kitsch used
so skillfully—I wish I
could do that—then he
starts to sing—so great—
I go down to hear him—
expecting a great
adoring crowd—but
he's singing in a half full
small theatre—a kind
of afterthought of a

theatre—we leave together
he puts his arm around
my shoulder—he looks
good—a bit beat up—
a bit older—but in full
possession of himself

***

I gave you my children
you said they were starving
and I gave you my knife
and the meat I was carving

Once I sang the ancient
now I sing the old
once I sang the sacrament
now I sing the mould

Old people roll their stockings up
while sitting on their beds
I need them on my mountain
I need their empty heads

Last year you dreamed
this year you killed
and now you are the ruler
of the kingdom that you willed

your love has traveled to the towns
you wanted her to leave for
and since you sent her there yourself
there's nothing left to grieve for

and, lovers of the future,
I know what I have done
I'm looking in the mirror
of the gun machine
yes baby
you're the queen of hearts.

You took my ring
and threw it in the garbage
I've been looking thru
the garbage ever since
if you find yourself
beside the city dump sometime
you'll find it covered
with my fingerprints

Your black suit
gleaming in my eye
like licorice

When you have broken down
you'll find me then
you'll find me on my knees
Fifth Avenue was an Indian path
& all of this was trees
Is this the way you wanted it
Did you choose to fall like this
with so little majesty

Rest here a little, pilgrim
I've been where it is summer
The crystals in your hair reveal
your road goes through the winter

the scratches on her movie
like rain that children draw

smiling to herself for herself
her own histories
her own grandmother
    remembering the incorruptible
    formula of her mouth
in nineteen sixty seven

You took my love
    and left it in the trash can
I've been looking thru
    the orange peels ever since
If some time you happen
    by the city dump
You'll find it covered
    with my fingerprints

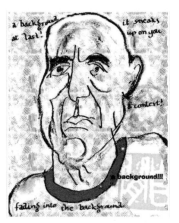

***

Saturday Morning
and the leaves are shining
and my small disease
is climbing the knob

Saturday Morning
and the ruins of Moscow
and the dark cement
is getting my job

Saturday Morning
and I'm sitting at the table
where I wrote
The Tower of Song

Saturday Morning
and I got nothing going
nothing going

nothing is wrong
All my secrets
I've told to the pillow
like a teenage girl
in a Motown song

And I'm burning
I'm burning to follow
my secrets
to the City of Death
on the outskirts of town

Saturday Morning
what was I saying
before the birds
interrupted my thought
I was thinking
of a room in Westminster
          room

with a woman from Hell
who thought she was hot

Saturday Morning
how long can I {you} wait
when it's clear that
you're serving your terror
and you're loving
all that you hate.

Saturday Morning
in the wonderful window
where the palm trees
tickle the wind

Saturday Morning
don't give up your courage
just breathe
and the worst will be over
but look it's coming again

I'm writing in the book that
you gave me
I'm so happy that we never
made love

Saturday Morning
and the leaves are shining
and my small disease
is climbing the knot
Saturday Morning
and the ruins of Moscow
and the dark cement
is getting my job
Saturday Morning
and I'm sitting at the table
where I wrote
The Tower of Song

Saturday Morning
and I got nothing going
nothing going

nothing is wrong
All my secrets
I've told to the pillow
like a Teenage girl
in a Motown song
And I'm burning
I'm burning to follow
my secrets
to the City of Death
on the outskirts of town

Saturday Morning
what was I saying
before the birds
interrupted my thought
I was thinking
of a room in Westminster
room

with a woman from Hell
who thought she was hot
Saturday Morning
how long can I wait
when it's clear that you
you're serving your terror
and you're loving
all those you hate.
Saturday Morning
by the wonderful window
where the palm trees
tickle the wind
Saturday morning
don't give up your courage
just breathe
and the worst will be over
but look it's coming again

***

I've driven a pin through your footprint
to make you stumble and swoon
I've covered it all with a detail
from somebody's old honeymoon

Nobody calls you who calls you
Nobody calls you but me
Nobody wants you who wants you
Nobody wants you but me

I'm lost in a shell with the ocean
I'm locked in an old honeymoon
You've driven a pin through my footprint
You've come after me with a tune

I've driven a shell through the ocean
I'm locked in an old honeymoon
I left some rain in your footprint

You gave me the words & the tune

lost in a spell that I started
to turn myself into a bone
locked in a room with the details
of somebody's old honeymoon

Lost in a spell that I started to
turn myself into a bone
you know that I'm just one of many
I hope you don't think I'm alone

Nobody wants you who wants you
Nobody wants you but me
The moon is after you, darling
It's wandered away from the sea

***

And O my heart
my lonely heart
how sweet
how sweet you sing

I knew that you
were lying
but I never

called you on it.

I told my brother
        what I heard
and he began to weep
I told my sister who whispered
"hush the baby is asleep"
I told the angels of the Lord,
they covered me with light
I told my heart, my heart did say:
"Be still with me tonight."

***

Oct 10, 2005

leave me out of all your histories
that's okay with me

I am as patient as the climate
I change when I am told

Thank you for
your gracious hospitality
my heart is light
when I recall the years
we have been together

as if you ever thought
that you were some kind
        of a teacher

when did that stupid idea
        take root?
when you had no other way
        to reach her?

***

Campanile   Nov 1, 2005

I just came back to say goodbye
It's true, it's true, we won
The bodies piled up tidal high
It wasn't that much fun

Been raining almost every day
We came here for the sun
We had that earthquake in L.A.
It wasn't that much fun

***

Nov 6, 2005

I was second to none
but I was never best
I was old and broke
so I could not rest

You can call it luck
be it good or bad
but you don't give up
when your heart is dead

it had to make you crazy
when you no longer had the money
or the youth
to bribe the referee

***

Soho Metro   April 8, 2006
Toronto

can't even tie your shoe
I look away
and cry for you

a mouse
with two matchsticks
and a bottle cap
is the drummer
for me

singing by myself

all morning
singing to myself
about Vanessa

I kissed you {once} hard
as if I were young
and you were so kind
to pretend that I was

and always that room
that window so wide
there was nothing beyond it
& no one inside

the story's been written
it's signed & it's sealed
you gave me a lily
but now it's a field

I don't know what happened
but who could have guessed
you'd leave us all hanging
that night that you left

Why didn't you tell me
that you had to leave
O noble departure
in silence and grief

***

May 27, 2006

and with me still
my darling friend
whose lips the decades
won't amend

my comfort in
the coming dusk
where hands can't feel
but memory must

my comfort in
the rising dust
where hands can't
so memory must

where flesh can't do
what memory must
the thrill of skin
in memory's trust

and even here
and even now
I can't regret
I don't know how

where lips can't drink
so memory must

your will to live
was too intense
you cut it down
it made no sense
when life betrayed you
with a yawn
you cut it down
lest it go on

I can't look back
or I will fall

time's good trick
reverse it all

lest suffering {torture} wear
its hideous grin
and bodies tear
and boredom wins

you cut away
the rotting wood
as any careful
gardener should

you kept your word
your deep concern

the winter's cold
the wood won't burn
you kept your word
your deep concern

fuck this valley
fuck this hill
where nothing works
and nothing will

fuck the bed
we lay upon
where nothing turned
my body on

baby you been gone a long time now
but you come to me in moments of unrest

and you hold my heart against
              your burning lips

and you tell me that my love
              has passed the test

You never really
          beat me up
but now and then
          you threatened
you were six foot two
          and some
and I was five foot
          seven

***

gonna live awhile
before I die
very peaceful
in the MRI

the boy
can't breathe
he can't even
go outside
it's the worst
attack of
breathless-
     ness

in a long long
2/18/03   time

The moon is full tonight
if only we could see it
and the garden
    filled with fragrance
if only we could
          breathe it

Every time I try to speak
It just doesn't come out right
Everything I try to say
it just sounds something like

that you were gone forever
and by your own dear hand

***

when I studied with the serpent
and sang confession to the trees
trying many sacraments from any hand
finding teachers anywhere
in all disguises insisting that I listen
to their daily talk
for the mystery it must disclose
and be left standing while
everyone else got high

The waitress came from Newfoundland
She said she knew the sea
I took her on a lonesome trip
until she cut me free

O darling you're waiting
for somebody's child
and once he was free
but now he is wild

And now that you're planning
to follow the sun
like a shadow of birds
or a crook on the run
you're travelling too light
for the seas you must swim
your thoughts are too deep
and your smile is too grim

You've broken the promise
you said in the barn
when you worried all night
while the killers were born
and your father did laugh
as he poured you some wine
then you shut the big doors
and lay down with the blind

You've broken the promise
you swore through your teeth
when you saw the words end
and the photographs weep
and nobody blames you
as the train pulls away
with its cargo of snow
for those glass paperweights

You've broken the promise
you said you would keep
but the paragraphs end
and the pictures still weep
like the sound of a storm

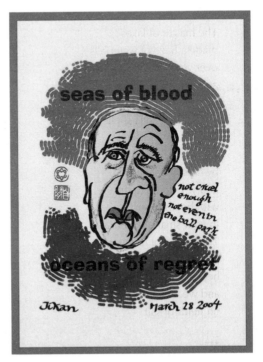

seas of blood

not cruel
enough
not even in
the ball park

oceans of regret

JiKan   march 28 2004

in a round paperweight
& nobody blames you
as the train pulls away
with the sound of a storm
in a round paperweight

***

after the poem
a little quieter
the people I imagine
waiting for me
are fast asleep
Marianne on Aylmer Street
enduring my hatred
until it rusted
and naming me higher and higher
until my view was wide
   enough to love her

The master of lakes
made a haze of waterfalls
over your shoulders
and you come to me
breasts soft as sand
and hard as snail shells
The master of traffic
has you followed ceaselessly
by crystal headlights
and you come to me
with beads of sap
in your small quick kisses
The master of farmyards
tethers newborn animals
beside your long legs
and we lie apart centuries
on fields of salt

some call it
the sap
some call it
the blood

189

***

She brought the telephone book
yellow against her green sleeves

and white shirted bosom
She stood in the doorway
talking to the engineer
whom she favoured of us all
After she left he leaned back
and relit a mexican cigar
and spoke about mixing vodka
with milk
Now my song is in the great speakers
and it is true as anything
that makes you dream

Have you suffered
for the sake of a bigger office
Have you betrayed your pain
which was meant
to bring you here

to this altar this sacrifice
these shackles of charity
Find your way to be among us
waiting for the bus
with the children gone
and no hope but in the sweetness of each other

***

I'm sitting here alone
    on Christmas day
I know, I know
    it shouldn't be this way
I been calling up some people
but everybody's out
& I been praying to the one
it's all about

if, this
morning,
you even
dare to
    speak

I don't know how I got this far
from everyone I love
or why I closed so many doors
what I was thinking of

***

Don't come to me
with your bright ideas
Don't talk to me
about the flowers
of this
or any other city
Your bright ideas
hurt my eyes
nor do I love
your rubber hose
the handcuffs
or the kitchen chair

***

because there was never anything better
I did in the human world
than to lie down in the fields of frankincense
with you

✿✿✿

Monday March 4[?], 2012   Tremaine Front Lawn

baby, don't remind me what it's like
the only thing I ever cared about
wasn't money
wasn't fame
wasn't family
wasn't art

baby, don't remind me what I miss
baby, don't remind me what I miss
I drove a thousand miles away from this

***

April 8ᵗʰ 2012   Front Lawn Tremaine

C'mon brother Trouble
when you gonna quit
you stole a bunch of money
I thought that was it

***

May 22, 2012   Tremaine   Tuesday afternoon

the troubles followed me
from bed to bed

i pitched my tent
wher'ere love led
no matter where
I slept and fed
the troubles followed me & {tailed me}
from bed to bed

I pitched my tent
wher'ere love led
the troubles followed
bed to bed

I moved away
when beauty fled
with beauty gone
the rest was dead
I knew too well
what Moses said
I must not touch
the body dead

with beauty gone
what's left is dead
I tried to do
what's hard to do
from showing up
to loving you

192

and loving you
that was a bitch
my self-defense
was getting rich

and buy off
your ugly greed
with every fucking thing
you need

the only news that isn't boring is the truth
but baby you ain't telling it
the only item you don't want to buy is love
but everybody selling it

        the sleek silver pen
it's supposed to write upside down
in space
        where I'm really going to have
nothing to write about

***

May 22, 2012   Tremaine   Tuesday afternoon

the troubles followed me
from bed to bed

i pitched my tent
wher'ere love led

no matter where
I slept and fed
the troubles followed me   tailed me
from bed to bed

I pitched my tent
where'ere love led
the troubles followed
bed to bed

I moved away
when beauty fled
with beauty gone
the rest was dead
I knew too well
what Moses said
I must not touch
the body dead

with beauty gone
what's left is dead
I tried to do
what's hard to do
from showing up
to loving you

July 10, 2002

all the leaves are shining
all the birds are singing
all the wind is blowing
all the bells are ringing
please don't make me say it anymore

I thought I'd go alone but
I'm glad I came with you
That's a rose
and that's a cactus
They're the same
but they're different too

***

I'll try to come home
once I've done what I must
which is what, please tell me
please tell me what

I forgot to mention
the moon and the trees
and the murderous blood
that runs through our veins

I forgot to mention
the pillars of gold
and the screams from the dungeon
the fingernails pulled

I forgot to mention
the blank space on my heart
where nothing is written
and the plan falls apart

I forgot to mention
the unmade bed
and the card on the doorknob
says Do Not Disturb

I forgot to mention
the skin on my head
hanging in folds disheveling my face
like an unmade bed

you climb up your ladder
of rumor and lies
you {slave} work for the master
you claim to despise

and you wave at the master

you never polished
your talent enough
content to remain
a diamond rough

I'm a weakling a failure
ashamed of myself / the cards I was dealt
my balls are so big
I can't buckle my belt

I {swear} strive to complete
before it's too late
some mission from G-d
I can't even locate

I can't seem to locate

get down on your knees
this ain't gonna pass
and pray there's no god
to punish your ass

I moan {boast} and I bitch
at the cards I was dealt
and my balls are so big
I can't buckle my belt

can't look in the mirror
I'm burning with shame

but I still like to boast
I'm ahead of the game

I'm tired of women
I don't trust the men

I'll try to come home
as soon as it's done
the mighty task
I can't even locate

I'll try to complete it
if it's not too late
the mission the sanctified mission
I can't even locate
that I can't locate

you gave away the factory
and you gave away my job
you said it's for the future {better}
and you said So help me God
you said one day I'd thank you
never gave nobody trouble
but I'm afraid it's gonna start

You gave away the future
you said I'd have to wait
It's for a better future
but the future's kind of late

I see you don't believe me
no matter what
          I do
my hand upon
          my mother's grave
but that ain't good
          enough for you

I tried
I don't know why
I didn't care why

flying a kite
no wind & no string
worse than "nothing to lose"
no juice to be hopeless
no heart to be sad
I tried in the wind
I tried in the sand
People turning into snakes
before my very eyes
I tried to hate
I tried to forgive
I tried baby
I tried to live

I tried to die
I tried to live

***

O
Copenhagen
Copenhagen
August 24
2012
Room 510
First Hotel

The red roofs
darkened by the rain
and the eternal
beginning of a cold

***

Field Commander Cohen is wounded
    call it age or love
the turret of his Sherman tank
    all slippery with blood
He who was a hundred lovers
    in a monk's disguise
is asking for a cup of water
    from a swarm of flies

O
Copenhagen
Copenhagen
August 24
        2012
Room 510
First Hotel
The red roofs
darkened by the rain
and the eternal
beginning of a cold

I am the song & not the singer
take his body
take his spirit

Not the boundary
but the centre

Save your anger, angels
the days are coming soon
when the earth will be
                    a mirror
the sun will be a cobweb
the moon will be a
                    spider
            coming near

call him Dylan
call him Jesus
call him Mister Rockefeller
I want to reach the people
that the master did not reach

***

maybe tomorrow will be better
and the banner raised again
for the sisterhood of women
& the brotherhood of men

***

just to breathe the air
and sip the rare
nectar of us together

to give you something
you might read
down the road or never

***

All of the lights
All of the sea broken lights
          of the river
All of the rhymeless thoughts of the hungry

***

Look at me I'm all alone
          I'm nobody's fool
I'm Nobody's Fool

and deeper than experience
I felt a woman presence
not like anyone I'd left
or anyone imagined.

***

I swear that I'll be true
to the uniform I wore
to the flag that I salute
and the promises I swore
I'll try to do my duty
just like I did before
but I can't hold you, baby,
to my heart no more

I know it's us or them
In the world that men call real
& a flower needs a stem
you can't grow these golden flowers
if the stems be not of steel
tho' the stem be made of steel
Can't blame you for the cruelty
when the killer's at the door
But I can't hold you, baby,
to my heart no more.

and I'm here between your safety
and the killer at the door

***

I bow my head
    in gratitude
to those who gave
    who give so much
so I can write
    my diary

I think, therefore I am
right up there with
    Mary had a Little Lamb

***

and ankle deep in a pool of blood
your uncle cries at last
"I don't care much for the movie
but the popcorn is unsurpassed"

& establish the terror
you long to command

***

When I saw
    how easily
the hand became
    a claw
I began to understand
the study of the law

***

Some people got the blues
Some people don't
Some people don't got food
That's the truth
I didn't say that it was news

I could not slip away
without telling you
that I died in Greece
was buried in that

place where the donkey
is tethered to the olive tree
I will always be there

To all of you
with whom I ate the fish
and clicked my glass
& never said a word
before I go
I want to say hello
from the stranger who
lived among you

***

out of the night
    the trees step forward
a solitary bird
    sharpens its song
on the stone-grey {mist} dawn

***

Her bread is very sweet
She baked it by herself
in an oven on a hill above the sea
an oven that I built
it took me several months
when I lived with her last year
when we weren't doing much
but keeping warm and near

We watched the different sailboats
of the rich and of the poor
the travelers from the cove
and the [?] from Gibraltar
We watched them
then a smoke ring that came from Lebanon

and we weren't doing much
so we waved at everyone

She phoned me from a long way off
just the other night
She's working in a private club
and she doesn't mind the life

She meant to talk 3 minutes
while they showed a silent movie
but we weren't very busy
so we spoke till it was bright

She asked if I was busy {happy}
and what the weather's like
we weren't doing very much
so we spoke till it was light

so we whispered half the night

I wasn't doing very much
& the weather's right
& the weather's been all right

She phoned me
        from a long way off
just the other night
She's working in a
        Playboy club
She doesn't mind the life
She asked if I was busy
& what the weather's like
I told her that I loved her
& the weather was all right

203

She phoned me from a long way off
just the other night
She's working in a private club
She doesn't mind the life
She asked if I was busy {happy}
& what the weather's like
I wasn't doing much
She spent a whole week's pay to learn
the weather'd been all right
& the weather'd been all right

I know that you can love me
if you'd only try
It's true I killed your brother
& I'm aiming at your eye
but these are only droplets
on the water wheel
save me all your energy
& tell me how you feel

Your songs are very sad
I hope that you will sing them
your poems are very long
I hope that you will bring them
Just leave them on my desk
I'll put your name in lights
& pick yourself a girl, may I
suggest the one in tights

***

first you were a clean-shaven fool
now you're a fool with a beard

***

what the old laws mean
why they distinguish between
what is clean
    and what is unclean

symbols in the flesh
have been given you
so that you may know
when you may approach
            one another

I write this on the
borderline

who insist that the
full moon should be
new and the new moon
should be full

I do not speak of sin
but only readiness and
hospitality & the wisdom
of restraint

***

you'll never understand
you don't need to understand
you're not supposed to understand
what it means to be a man
to feel this overwhelming love
to be so awkward
        and so tough
and to know it's not enough
to say I want you baby
            I want you
with my dying breath

***

Aug 21, 1989 Mt. Baldy

I take the train
but I do not dare
to really look at anybody
riding with me there
some are poor some are rich
some are black some are white
but I don't know which is which
in my secret life

& I'll never be able
to bring a little baby
from my belly to the cradle
so what if there's a war
so what if there's a fight
there is no [finer?] sight
for ever & forever
nothing can be better
than the man and the
        woman together

***

Beautiful are the nights in Canaan
How long will you live in my heart,
    O homeland
Sleep my darling girl
A girl is expecting her lover
She lies in bed listening
      to the train

Under a greenwood tree
two boys are sitting, talking
about a maid, and nothing
else matters to them.

I change my dwelling places
and change my haunts and
wander from country to country,

the little silence whose
name is Abishag

My mother's holy hands
are mending my shirt.
Come to me or leave me waiting
I don't care no more

I've waited like a month
    and I waited like a stone

I've waited on a feather
    and I've waited on a storm

I've waited like a mountain
    and I've waited like a door

I've waited on the bridges
    that the rivers washed away

I waited like a bridegroom
    with another man's bouquet

I waited for your beauty
　　to be given to the rain

I stood outside {beyond} my tears {sorrow}
　　like a statue in the rain

I folded {up} my heart
　　and I cut it with your love
a string of paper dolls

I'm standing here
　　in the blinding light
I don't know what to do
my nakedness

she was
protected
by rays
of light

I'm standing here
　　in the blinding light
I've come to the end of the line
& my nakedness cries out for you

cries out like a drunk
　　for his bottle of wine

I'm standing here
　　　in the blinding light
& I don't know what to do
the blinding light
　　of what I lost

when I walked away from you

the blinding light
　　when you're stalled at night

O baby forgive me
　　the things that I did
& forgive me the things
　　　　that I said
cries out like
a man that is buried alive
like a voice that cries
out from the dead

Forgive me what I did to you
Forgive me what I said
My heart & my soul
& my nakedness
cries out to be comforted
cries out like a man
who's been buried alive
cries out like a voice
from the dead

so let's not tear the past apart

we shared the darkness
from the start

I'm an evil son of a bitch

I was born in the heart of the bible
& I know the holy pitch
I could sell an angel paper wings
I'm an evil son of a bitch

Not for all the jasmine
          in Moscow
not for all the singing
          in New York
not for all the broken hearts
          in Bloomingdale's
not for all the telephones
          in Long Island
not for all the blue
          in Istanbul
not for all the shoes
          in Bloomingdale's
not for all the rags
          in Lebanon

not for all the wax
          in Notre-Dame
not for all the books
          in Jerusalem
not for all the glass ice
          in a summer

Beautiful are the nights in
                Canaan

How long will you live in
                my heart,
    O homeland

Sleep my darling girl

A girl is expecting her
                lover.
She lies in bed listening
        to the train

I change my dwelling
                places
and change my haunts and
wander from country to
country,

the little silence whose
name is Abushay

My mother's holy hands
    are mending my shirt.

Under a greenwood tree
two boys are sitting, talking
about a maid, and nothing
else matters to them.

Come to me or leave me
                    waiting
I don't care no more

I've waited like a month
        and I waited like a
                        zturo

I've waited on a feather
        and I've waited on a stone

I've waited like a mountain
        and I've waited like a
                            door

                    uh
I folded my heart
        and I cut it with your love
a string of paper dolls

I've waited on the bridges
        but the waves washed
                            away

I waited like a bridegroom
        with another man's bouquet

I waited for your beauty
        to be given to the rain
        boyfriend   sorrow
I stood outside my tears
        like a statue in the rain

***

you're standing tall
you're hanging tough
but I know you're feeling bad
It's easy to see
that a good woman's love
is something that you never had
so I'm gonna take pity on the boy tonight
I'm gonna do you a favour gonna do it right
I'm gonna see that you're fed
I'm gonna put you to bed
& then I'm gonna drive you mad

***

I don't know who you're looking at
It must be someone else
I'm only here a minute
then I go somewhere else

I'm talking to myself
I'm living {visiting} at the clinic
just talking to myself
I'm only here a minute
then I go somewhere else

do not cry "heal me lord"
the lord is broken
        heal the lord
so come my children
        and confess
when we are more
the lord is less

I just can't pretend no more
that I'm your loving man
I just can't pretend no more
that I really give a damn
It's just too hard to make you smile
and too dangerous to bring you down

You got love
you got sex
you got nothing to lose
you got death
     in your mind
like a root

you got stuff
it's a mess
you got no one to choose
you got breasts
     on your chest
you're a brute

I never went back
I never came home
I waited all night
for you to come home
or someone like you
I couldn't keep touch

I don't know about tomorrow
but I know what's coming next
I was broken when I met you
I was broken when I left
I couldn't do it living
but I love you with
     my dying breath

I came here for the healing
How about you?
The god of love is broken
the god of hatred too

Every time I touched you
My oh My oh My

That night you let me touch you
I thought that I would die

i wasn't really sure
i was allowed in there
but i thought the rules
were somewhat ambiguous
and if discovered
i could justify my presence

there was a narrow camp bed
close to the door
with fresh sheets
and a light blanket
I snuggled into
the bed and began to listen
intently to the confession
the young woman was
making to her therapist

I don't remember what she was
saying but she stopped
abruptly and said:
"Leonard Cohen is listening
to us"

It was night & it was raining
and the pizza never came

I'm troubled by war
I'm troubled by peace
Can't they think of anything else

***

I am a souvenir of creation
The ringed wife is a souvenir
of first dip in the private morning
pool when you sank like a
fish hook through the layered
mirrors of self-love

O God change your name
in my heart
        but the chairs
        once with straw now
        with yellow red plastic
        woven
        the new Blue Tops of
        outdoor tin tables
        Fresh Paint!

Not today
I knelt in that certainty

***

and you put your baby
number nothing
on the waiting list

and long nights alone
with the angels of the Lord
I put the books of love aside

the young dancers
who have never
thought about death
and the older ones who have
to lie once more
in the proud arms of one
who has never thought
        about death

I look out at the hillside
all silver and silent
its beauty is signed in the air

Then night comes a stealing
the shapes of our feeling
the whole world is melting in fire
I'm there, I'm finally there

***

like David bent down
in the darkness of love
I call out your name
and I ask to be done
with this burden of heart
with this pride of despair
with this shame
that the heart cannot {bear}

to the realms of despair

like David bent down
on his bed of all despair
I come to you now
I call out your name
I ask to be done
with this darkness of love
with this burden of heart
with this shame
that the heart cannot bear

like David bent down
in the darkness of his love
I call to you now
{from} the place of despair
I call on your name
& I ask to be done
with the burden of heart

like David bent down
to the darkness of his love
with his kingdom of dust
with his crown of despair
with no hope from the night
with no word for his prayer

like David bent down
in the realms of despair
with no hope from the night
with no word for his prayer
he comes to you now
he calls on your name

he asks to be done
with the darkness of love
with his burden of heart
with his shame

from both sides of the battleground
from liberty from love

like David bent down
to the darkness of his love
with no river below
and no light from above
and he cries out your name
from the place of despair
for the burden of heart
{from his high}
{heavy chain}
that he cannot repair
for the burden of shame {heart}
which is there, which is there
{for the darkness of love}
for the shame
which his {the} heart
cannot bear

like David bent down
in the darkness of love
with no kingdom or crown
& no light from above
& he cries out your name
from the place of despair
for the burden of shame
which he cannot repair

& he cries out your name
with no heart for the prayer
for the burden of shame
in the place of despair

for the burden of heart
which is there, which is there
for the shame
that the heart cannot bear

I am the light of
        my generation
and the radio
and the refrigerator

with no kingdom below
& no crown from above
and he cries out your name
from the place of despair
for the darkness of heart
which he cannot repair
beyond all repair
for the burden of shame
which is there, which is there
for the shame which the heart
cannot bear

look see how he wakes
hear how he speaks
& he tries to raise his hands to the lord

the world begins to wait for thee
I have it deep inside of me
like uncreated angels see
the absence of eternity

the world begins to wait for thee
I have it deep inside of me
a longing that could only be
the absence of eternity

like David bent down
        in the darkness of shame
I come to you now
I cry out your name
with no hope for the day
with no heart for the prayer

Renew the name that
        sorrow has forgotten
Speak again
and raise creation up

Renew the name
& stand your singer up

and a painful silence mock
all the parliament of thought

I don't want to be here
anymore

and the silence gathered
round to mock
all the parliament of thought

Find me here

I can't cry out
I have no word
And in this place
was never heard

In the absence of
human actions fail & rot
around the parliament of thought

Pretending to stand
like a man in the place
where there is no light
and there is no face

If I speak to you, if I try,
one word, one breath at a time;
if I listen between the words,
if I go slowly,
will you come to this place
you have cleaved for my
doubting

If I try to speak

I beg you to come to this place
I beg you
with all the ugliness at my disposal
I offer this headache
and my accomplice dream women
I beg you with the headache
in my right eye
I beg you with the fly
that has chosen my lips
to fertilize
I beg you with the interesting news
of manure & unemployment

what are you keeping there,
what have you hidden away
that is so precious to the
darkness; so heavily guarded,
so furtively {defiantly} held,
now furtively, now defiantly
held; your power magic,
your heavy-machine, to
your axioms of strategy
iron mask
    your victory

your victory, your
supremacy, preening
itself in a basin of vomit,
waiting, waiting until
you say, now

your victory creature,
chained to the coming
opportunity, preening
itself in a basin of
vomit, waiting to spring,
waiting until they turn
their backs, and you say,
now!

Chained to your secret place
feeding on the spirit carrion,
they wait to be unleashed
I heard them singing
        just the other day
pouring out their hearts
                in wild dismay

their voices sweet with
        what they could not say
the song of Ages on their
                lips of clay

The beasts go roaming free

Come my love, my holy one
enter on the carpet of my longing
Baby, don't be sad
the dust is all my doing
The wind and the umbrellas
come from stores
the flags from the nation
but your absence comes
from a terrible sleep
under a huge museum
Enter the moth holes
        of my longing

Like David bent down
in the darkness of love
I call out your name
and I ask to be done
with this burden of heart
with this field of despair
with this shame
that the heart cannot
bear

---

to the realms of despair

Like David bent down
to the darkness of his love
with his kingdom of dust
write his crown of despair
with no hope from the night
with no word for his prayer

Like david bent down
in the realms of despair
with no hope from the night
with no word for his prayers
he comes to you now
he calls on your name
he asks to be done
with the darkness of love
with his burden of heart
with his shame

Like David bent down
on the bed of all despair
I come to you now
I call out your name
I ask to be done
with the darkness of love
with this burden of heart
with this shame
And the heart cannot bear

Like David bent down
in the darkness of his love
I come to you now
from the place of despair
from
I call out your name
& I ask to be done
with the burden of heart

---

from both sides of the battleground
for liberty from love

Like David bent down
to the darkness of his love
with no river below
and no light from above
and he cries out your name
from the place of despair
for the burden of heart
that he cannot repair
for the burden of shame
which is there, which is there,
for the shame
which his the heart
cannot bear

some cut high
every calm

for the darkness
of love

***

I had a plan
   I was moving away

Far from the failure
   and stress every day

***

May 2, 2011
1995[?]

the Great Convulsion
        coming

we're nothing like the ant hill
we're not a hive of bees
Behold! the good ship
     "Free Will"
as she's tossed on mighty seas
        mighty seas

you can always depend
   on me
I'm going to come down
      on the side of mercy

I'm going to come down
    on the side of love

The Great Convulsion
        coming

I'm going to run like hell
      from the general terror

and hide like a bell
       in the panic

I'm going to run like hell
      from the usual
           Titanic
& hide like a bell
      in the general panic

***

Where are your friends
         my darling
wait they'll be coming thru
my friends are back there
        dancing
That's what I like to see them do

I thought I heard them
            weeping
just before the rain
you might have heard them
            weeping
but they're dancing once again

What are the ladies wearing
back there on the floor
the old forbidden clothing
that the Emperor once wore

Can't we go back my darling
I've been away too long
Why did you leave us dancing
in the middle of the song

I thought the dance was over
when all the rain came down
then you must die my darling
on the other side of town

I like the other side of town
It has a perfect view

***

In this writing
we do not look out the window
we do not wait
for the Swedish girl
to walk down the aisle
and we do not think about
her faded gold face
which is her nakedness
we do not speculate
on the superior style
and the origin
of his old sun clothes

***

I was talking to Ron
when the women were gone
and the men were out killing for love
we were touring the north
with the songs of my youth
for the last time. Enough is enough

Dear Hatred
Dear Heart-Broken Olivia
in the Xenias Melathron
eating an apple
forever on my Grecian urn
Dear Princess Zina
I shaved my head for you
Now you send me printed letters
asking me to buy you a monastery

Dear Accident Helga
of my sunstroke at noon
later the dog-like companion
of fork-bearded Sascha
cool candlelight of ignitable icicles
in your cheeks and eyes
nothing at all between us
except my kneeling for you now

I gave all my money
          to charity
I gave all my clothes
          to the poor
I followed after one
          who was saving me
I thought that he was
          very brave and pure

My name is John the Baptist
I had my glory
          on the riverbed

how can you leave me
you must not leave me
even to masturbate
even to eat or to pray
the Levi's shirt on the back of the chair
the hotel where the King of Hanover
died in 1878
the poem of Paris
to break my heart when I'm eighty
how can you leave me
how can you desert this work
to carry a small-caliber revolver
with which to threaten
your New York business partner
the mind of a rich human being
you must not leave me

Look at yourself
sitting on the wooden steps
in the morning sunlight
you are wearing an old white shirt
from the button-down days,
sandals you bought with Meredith
when you lived with her in Mexico,
corduroys become work pants
from two weeks of painting

Sitting on the wooden steps
in the morning sunlight
trying to learn how to die

Goodnight, goodnight you evil ones
may you rest at last
There is a happy ending
to all the bloody past

This is the night of July 20, 1972

***

Dear Steve

Thanks for helping me
across the road

The last fellow tried that
they had to scrape off the corner

Since I no longer wish to explain myself
I have become a stone
Since I no longer long for anyone
I am not alone

***

to V.R   Jan 19, 2002

and it won't be wine and roses
from now until the end
but it will never, it will never
be that dark again

***

May 10, 2002

you said I was lying
you called all my tricks
but you never did nothing
your lips couldn't fix

and all you want to do
is breathe easy
   be in any place
   hang alone
      or with people
but breathing easy
all I ever wanted
   that's the truth
but now I'm out of breath
which is why I work
otherwise I wouldn't work
I'd just lie around
breathing easy

the boy
can't breathe

he can't even
go outside
it's the worst
attack of
  breathless-
    ness

in a long long
2/18/03 time

***

I put my voices in your life
you can listen without stopping
you can listen
           in your car tonight

I sang for you Nico
your face was in my song
I knew what beauty was
the lines of the moon
on your mouth
as I entered my song

***

I never got the girl I wanted
did you, Jack?

***

I never held you in my arms
I never watched you go to school
Sometimes I think of you
The child I never had
The child I never knew
Sometimes I long for you
my baby, oh my baby
my lullaby in blue

It's lost in a rush of emptiness

I cross my arms against my breast
& I'm lost in a nest of emptiness
& you're lost in me, you're lost so deep
that I rock myself
    & I rock you to sleep
I do, my child I really do
my lullaby, my lullaby in blue

& it's lost in me, it's lost so deep
I cross my arms
against my breast
and I sing you to sleep
I do, my child, I really do
my lullaby, my lullaby in blue

***

Nov '88
Someone that
       who I never knew
my lullaby in blue

and I'll never know
what my mother knew

***

And all my brave companions
    where are they?

Working for the women in
    the sad café—
No wonder there is money
    on the throne
No wonder there is oil
    Babylon

Here with the
devil
here with the
lord

my grandfather appeared
and demanded:
"What have you
done with my
books? My
'Lexicon of
Hebrew
Homonyms'
my Thesaurus
of Talmudic
Interpretations
my unfinished
'Dictionary'?

here with the
plowshare
here with the
sword

here with the glory
here with the hoof
here with the wisdom {knowledge}
here with the proof

***

7715 Woodrow Wilson
May 12 1976

quickly quickly
give Jerusalem
to God

***

Swimming Club
Thursday March 10, 2:30 pm

I lost my job today
I hoisted up the sun
to start the break of day
I was a very special one
but I lost my job today

I lost my job today
I was hired by the sun
hired to guide it on its way
I was that very special one
but I lost my job today

I lost my job today
I'd been hired by the sun
to guide him on his way
to hold Him to His way
I was that very special one
but I lost my job today

I think we're going to see some action here

Some sunlight is going to fall on the matter

A resolution A defining moment has been reached

It is emanating from the imperishable stuff beneath the loose flesh of ambiguity

2/5/03

229

I lost my job tonight
I'd been hired by the moon
to sweep Her beauty bright
I worked every afternoon
but I lost my job tonight

***

now you know how wide
the net of suffering's cast
nor will the teachers from Tibet
or the rabbis from New York
assuage the thirst that rises
from the throat of loneliness
here behind the nest of sorrow
waits the one who lets you live and die
whose company is sweet as hell
and mightier than heaven

when your fingers are
too bent to seize the pieces
of the jigsaw puzzle
and you don't really care
what the picture's going to be
you may hear the little
useless song
of the one who's given up

I've been {was} here too long
But I've crossed the line
but the train's on time
and the will is strong
for it is not mine

***

I have witnessed many great events, some of which were sorrowful: the birth of
children, the death of friends, the ends of time & the intermediate wildernesses.
A chill goes down my spine and up, when I reflect how graciously I have been
placed in the mazes of creation. My beloved is with me, the wife of my youth,
and in the midst of suffering, when it is our lot, if I remember to incline my self
toward the source of light, I know that I have never strayed too far from my

bridal days. As it was promised, I have inherited the gates of my enemy, and I fear with him, rejoice with him, at the irresistible tides of majesty that sweep across the world.

I am on one side
but I affirm both sides
in this war
that is not why we are losing
we are not losing
but that is why the victory is slow
Patience is our weapon,
prayer our strategy,
and sacrifice our understanding
of the times.
Take heart, you who have
not been gathered yet,
watch for the banner we have
raised,
and come to us when the walls
of your sanctuary begin to
give against the weight of tears

With you again, old friend
with you again
sweeten now our company
soften now the rain

Remember Valentin
The woman of the quarrel
She is concealed from us
who was so beautiful

But why the silence now
the look of bitter knowing
just because it's getting dark
& we don't know where we're going

We often have meandered
such an afternoon
something will turn up
if it's only the April moon

I agree, it's getting worse
and they're stacking up the chairs
that's what comes from choosing life
above the enemies' prayers

There are bugs
in my crotch hair
but I can't find them
contrary to the opinion
of those who have inspected me
I know they're there
They picnic in the thickets
where once was concentration
and the stillness of desire

I feel ridiculous
in my grey suit
and my pomaded hair
all groomed for love
while the vermin
swarm between my thighs
and lower and higher

(This has been going on
for a long time now
It has driven me to prayer
I never thought I was an animal
I never thought I have free will
Now I'm stuck with both realities)

The saxophone
establishes a mood
the girls, dressed for the evening,
come in & out of the café
and the rabbis sit down beside me
for a good lazy talk

Is this my destiny
to be so attractive & unavailable
The rabbi is deep, but my thought
is deeper, and scratching doesn't help

O insect host, the backsliders were
burned to save them from the
flames of hell—will
your living filth prevent {forestall} the
grave's corruption

***

he said, I think
I know your story
you were in love
with Ava Gardner
or someone like her
you were as lonely
as Frank Sinatra
or someone like him

Now that China's
fallen out of heaven
& rots with Russia
in the mortal pit
and Marx himself
is just a Jewish dreamer
which even Frenchmen
finally do admit

I put my elbows
on the roof of its car
I never want to drive again
& I never want to
feel so bad
about anyone as
I feel about you
I never want
I don't want to feel
like I do
    when I talk to you

I'd rather be dead
like the rose
that I left on the heater

***

You can see it
on their faces
you can feel it
in their stride
It's the changing
of the races
It's the changing
of the guard

New York City
to San Francisco
Puerto Rico
Angelino
Fundamental
Fruit of Islam
Heavy Metal

Nothing heavy
Nothing special
Just the music
Just the people

Covered wagons
in a circle
From Moscow
To L.A.
Don't worry
'bout the missiles
Just point them
the other way

Beethoven
and the Bible & Chuck Berry
Shakespeare
and MGM
Farewell to
New York City
Farewell to
Bethlehem

***

I don't need no
    midnight promise
I don't need no
    wedding ring
Just don't ask me
    how I got here
Don't ask me
    anything

But if you buy me
    a yellow sweater
I will love you
    till the end of time

I don't want to
    ask the gypsy
what the future
    has in store
I don't want to
    ask the doctor
what these little
    pills are for

I've been looking
    out the window
at the people
    passing by
I don't ask myself
    a question
I don't even
    wonder why

All the stores are
    filled with songs
All the streets are
    paved with gold
When it comes to
    telling secrets
I don't tell them
    till they're old

if only
she hadn't

Saturday 1:40 am December 27, 2003

I sincerely hope
you have not
come to believe,
that simply because
you ran off & got
married behind
my back, you
are somehow
entitled to keep

my tape measure

***

You must have heard it in my voice
the sound that I no longer love you
I would never disguise that sound
I would never do that to you
O shining one
you have moved beyond my love
you have turned your face to others
I was not strong enough for this test
I turned away
I wear an iron collar
and I give my chain to anyone
but I never pretend that they are you
O shining one
who held my spirit like a match
in your cupped hands
while I thought I was warming you
O shining one
who teaches with her absence

***

I asked for the check
I'm having too much fun
Several grandmothers
are winking at me
I may do something I'd regret

We will be forgiven
the crummy things
we did to one another
because we
didn't enjoy them

We'll be leaving now
we'll be leaving
for a good long time
and we want to say goodnight
we want to say goodnight
we want to say farewell

We had a little love
we had it for a while
It wasn't quite enough
but thank you anyhow

Thank you for your kindness
in the field
and thank you for your kindness
in the room

The horses ran away
but we were not to blame
and when they
turned so beautiful
in their silver flight
it wasn't our idea
at least it wasn't mine

I want to be with other people
now I'm growing old
I want to be another drunk
who's given up the bottle
I want to watch the lonely men
who still go out with women
I want to see the bridal gown
cover up the sequins
This is my very night of nights
the past was a rehearsal

how come you look so good tonight
I thought you've given up the fight
your shoulders bare
your eyes so bright
how come you look so good tonight

***

I watch the crowd passing
and I wonder when
they will throw off my burden
and choose me again
for I was a king
in the ancient domain
I ruled over no one
and overthrew pain

My name it is hidden
my friends live alone
I know who they are
when they ring on the phone
And we don't say a word
we just breathe thru the line
and we never untie
what is yours what is mine

***

To Tinkie

you walked me to school
you slept under my bed
you watched me masturbating
with interested eyes
you protected me
from my enemy loneliness
even in your old age
you greeted me
every time I saw you
you left the house
and died in the snow

under the neighbour's porch
and you were lost
until the late summer
when I was out of town
and they cleared away
your body
I didn't believe them
and even today
I stop every scottie
to claim you back

***

HOUSE

it's my house of olden marriage
nothing much to say
the price of love forbidding
desire had to pay

was sitting in the kitchen
where often I was served
by one who could not stay with me
I said goodbye in words

my house of olden marriage
we were the keepers proud
she of what I could not be
me of whom she mustn't love

was sitting in the kitchen
talking to myself
which lately had come down to me
from off the trinket shelf

239

and this is made to keep him strong
who is my lord and trust
and this is made to keep her free
from all the household dust

***

True love is what happens between two people
who no longer need to know each other

***

but you chose me
   a young lieutenant
      in the palace
a very minor figure
   in the general scheme
of cosmic entertainment

I press my uniform
      my trousers & my shirt

my holster gleams
   in the moonlight
I wait for you in the botanical gardens
which is locked at night
but I have obtained a key
and I wait for you
beside the rows
of night blooming jasmine

Your starless nights
      your lipstick life
you work
as a silhouette

I was just a minor figure
   in the junta

your strapless night
   your cigarette
the moon behind
   your deco silhouette

The colonel wanted you
   as did the Minister
         of the Interior

I was just a minor figure
                in the junta
a lieutenant
        in the palace guard
I cannot forget
        that lonely summer
{and the sky} and that night
so luminously starred

It is not for me
    to explain or justify
the history of mankind
It is not my place
    to make a statement
I was educated by the Jesuits
    and the Sanhedrin
but no one could explain to me
the screaming from the basement

Adolf Hitler Mussolini
Stalin Mao Tse Tung
I wasn't born a devil
but I dreamed of being one

I still get many offers
but there's someone I must thank
All of us were robbed
& Dylan was the Bank

The leading man
the leading man
        the man I'll never be
he stole my woman
        in New York
and my horse
        in Tennessee

***

Studio   May 24 '03

How long
     will you go on pretending
there's something
     you know how to fix
How many more digital shots will you {edit?} take
   of the helpless, the old and dead & the sick
Will you ever stand up and be seen
     by the sultan, the slaves, and the secret police
     and when are you going to
stand up and be seen
When are you going diving for coins
     to stop swimming
in the lakes and the sewers of filth

When are you going to help someone out
who's certainly
     going to be killed

When are you going to be fingered
              and be stripped

by a dreamer who's aching
     to kick out your teeth

how long will you go on diving
    for changes in the sewers of filth

***

The truth minus 7%

He only kissed you
        on the cheek
and he only touched your hand
you say that nothing happened
and I'll let your story stand
That's a {mighty?} big bunch of roses
that "nothing happened" sent
but I thank you for telling
       the truth to me

242

The truth minus seven
                    Percent

***

Frankfurt Airport Feb 19, 2002

I'd like to pray
five times a day
    in fact I do
I'd like to live
as though G-d lived
    through me and you
    in fact I do

***

Mumbai
[?] Jan 3, '03

We made a little garden
in the middle of L.A.
so our hearts
    they wouldn't harden

& our spirits
            they could play

***

Annie's asleep by the fireside
That's my book in her hand
That's my thorn in her side.
We loved that way
"   "   "   "
"   "   "   "

for more than a year, I'd say.

***

I used to have a life
        I was living at the centre

There's people {places [?] went} that I love
& there's women that I know

A waitress called me sir
then she called me Leonard
I like the edge it's better
    than the centre

***

It has waited until this night
concealed in tears, and {the} lines I've
conferred, and broken promises
It believes, though I do not believe
It waits, though I have given up waiting
It is strong, though I am not
Everything else I have misused and squandered
because I could not lie about this love
It summons me, though I have no courage
and it bids me to say these words
to you:
I have waited for you all my life
I have never given myself to another

You are my first love and my last

***

I'm trying to catch the future
I don't know which way it goes
I've got a stomach full of ouzo {sunlight}
and a sterling silver nose
My guitar is very quiet
There's a song it likes to tell me
My songs are like the stars
They {just} control they don't compel me
And my love is blonde and ancient
I met her by the sea
She was putting things together
and she needed some of me
Come back here when you're thirsty
she whispered thru a wave

Then she took me down a thousand feet
to the midwife in my grave
and she saved us in a grave

There's a song it needs to tell me
My songs are only planets
They control, they don't compel me
and my love is blonde and ancient
I met her by the sea
She was putting things together
and she needed some of me
Come back here when you're thirsty
She whispered through a wave
Then she took me down a thousand feet
and sewed us in a grave
I have my hand on both our bodies
It's the bridge I cannot find
through the razorblades and daisies
to the birth we leave behind

***

Dec 18th 2011   Palisades

I am a living statue
I moved for you
when you gave me
a quarter euro
My closest friend
sprayed me bronze
early this morning
when it was
      still dark

I am the best
      living statue
in Germany
I make a fortune
No one is as still
      as I am
I hover over
      my bronze body

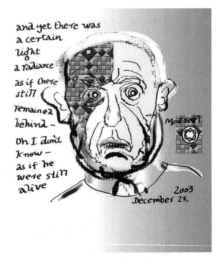

and yet there was
a certain
light
a radiance
as if there
still
remained
behind –
Oh I don't
know –
as if he
were still
alive

Montserrat

2003
December 23,

245

Dec 18ᵗ 2011   Palisades

I am a living statue

I moved for you

when you gave me

a quarter euro

My closest friend

sprayed me bronze

early this morning

when it was

        still dark

I am the best

      living statue

in Germany

I make a fortune

No one is as still

      as I am

I hover over

     my bronze body

like a bird

above her nest

The living statue

    ignore the compliments

the propositions

    the marriage

       proposals

She is safe

    and beautiful

       forever

even when my friend

helps me off

    my pedestal

and we go home

and I am alone

   in the shower

like a bird
above her nest

The living statue
   ignore the compliments
   the proposition
   the marriage
      proposals

She is safe
   and beautiful
         forever
even when my friend
helps me off
   my pedestal
and we go home
and I am alone
   in the shower

***

and Nico was blond
and Dylan was found
   in a pit he alone had descended
and there he unfurled
for the sake of the world
   the bright flag so long undefended

***

I've had it
I've had it with you
and the kid
and the farm
and the job
and the war
and the debt
and the bullshit
I read
in the palm of my hand
and what did you do
with my god

247

and my church
and my car
and my dick
was I supposed
            to like

living on my fucking knees?

of course I don't
say this to anyone
especially {not to} my wife
especially my kids
and not to anyone
bigger or stronger
or the boss
or the sadist in
charge of my teeth {mind}

and it all looks
so peaceful
when you're not
hunting for pussy
or sucking up to
the lord
I advise you all to
get tired and old
and bored
cranky and bored

and then the voice
is heard
deeper than the world
you may need acid
to hear it, or weed

never did it for me
and I took (maybe)
a hundred trips at
least

***

and I sought my beloved
when I was trying to make my marriage {work}
move from islands to cities & back again
when I was trying to make my marriage work
but I could not find my beloved

And you made me use words
like husband and wife
to cross a border to cash a cheque
words that armed my solitude
against my daily life

you wrote your poems
without the recognition
without the prize of women
without the sting of fame
not even for the name of poet
did you labour on the empty page
and just the news of you
silenced many a juke-box

I declared my high intention to be free
I cut myself shaving

***

go tell your brother
the family is no more
go tell your baby sister
she's nothing but a whore
go tell the Angels of the Lord
there is no God above
go tell your heart of longing
that there's no such thing as love

I told my brother
            what I heard
& he began to weep
I told my sister, she said Hush
the baby is asleep
I told the angels of the lord
they covered {blinded} me with light

I told my heart, my heart did say
Be still with me tonight

O man of flesh, my heart did say
as I went through the night
prepare yourself for sorrow
& prepare for sweet delight
There came a tide of suffering
which I could barely stand
you must sacrifice your sorrow
on the altar of delight
and I went down in tears
There came a dark indifference
which seemed to last for years
There came a spring where nothing grew
There came a summer with no sun
There was no crystal in the snow
No harvesting for anyone

There was no crystal in the snow
No fragrance in the spring
No summer with its naked dance
No autumn harvesting
I tried to cry, {my eyes were sealed} there were no tears
I tried to laugh, there was no scorn
I tried to run, there was no road
I tried to die, I was not born
I pinned across a piece of meat
hanging in the abattoir
I struggled for a woman's touch

I pinned across a piece of meat
& feeding on a {barren} star
I struggled for a woman's touch
for solace {comfort something} in the abattoir

The boredom of her {our} company
The sting trance of her {our} embrace
whiled away the outlines
hanging face to face
O let it end, O solace me
now

let me surrender now
O make it clear what you forbid
and what you allow

The boredom of our company
The trance of our embrace
These were the very hooks
            that held us
hanging face to face

And many times I begged my heart
let me surrender now
I'll put aside what you forbid
I'll take to me what you allow

And then the laughter in the air
you cannot yield, there is no war
you cannot lose, there is no game

Now lest I be the juda's lamb
& lead you to the knife
This is not a parable
It's but a human life
The man who tells this story
he is sitting on a bed chair
wondering where to go and how
to get from here to there

He says this as a caveat
to the {blind} ears of youth
that there is the stink of beauty
above {the} corpse of truth

But now the night is ending
for one listening to his heart
        for this listener of the heart
The baby's crying for {singing in the [?]} crib
The lovers break apart
My sister heats {a} bottle
& my brother starts the car
The Angels dress as humans
to be with us where we are

The baby's singing in the crib
The lovers break apart

But only music has the power
so put your head upon the stories

I've grown old
in a hundred ways
but my heart is young
& still it plays
on the theme of love
on the theme of death
o close it plays
as my very breath
they rise & fall
with my very breath
my son goes back
and forth on a swing
and then he wears
a wedding ring
he works a mighty
task and then
my son is one
with me again

In a mother's womb
my daughter stirs
and then the moving
child is hers
and then heroic
duties call
and the deepest
womb of all

and many a bitter
night went by
that death would win
& love would try

and many a bitter
night goes by

that death must win
and love must try
sweet
and my darling removes {unlocks}
the clasp of her hair
and many the blessings
of sweet repair
till she
{my darling} unfastens
the clasp of her hair
and many the blessings
of sweet repair
till she unpins
her [wigs?] black hair

***

Now I am not your father
but since your father's dead
I'll tell the bedtime story
before you go to bed

So come and gather round me
but do not sit too near
The closer that you sit to me
The less that you will hear

Among my stories there is one
you've never heard before
though all I've said goes round it
like the apple round its core

It is the story of a love
I had for one of you
when you were neither seed nor child
and I was nothing too

Forbidden to be spoken by me
or anyone
but now the seal is broken
and the story has begun

And who forbid the telling
is a question you may pose
It was he who hated nakedness
and made us all wear clothes

***

They are far ahead of me
the true writers
with whom I once paced myself
tarrying with women and riches
and problems of the Way
I fell behind
losing all but the original uneasiness
This is my fourth day
without cigarettes or coffee
my eye on Shakyamuni and St. Francis
as it was once
on Flaubert and William Butler Yeats
and I still have this ugly feeling
that I will reform the world

***

I know you don't believe me
& that's why you have to split
you're looking for a peaceful place
& this ain't exactly it

So I'll drive you to the station
& I'll put you on the train
There's one that sinks in the ocean
& there's one that stops in Maine

I used to travel like a fool
when I was middle-aged
but then I settled down with you
when settling was the rage

I'm glad you left that photograph
of you & me at Harvard
you didn't really leave it but
I fished it from the garbage

***

August 1985

They took me to the Holy Land
and up to the Wall of Sorrow
I said, these stones are made of sand
and they won't be here tomorrow

They {took me} to Mount Everest
and they pointed to the summit
I said I am impressed
but it's just another limit

***

I saw you on the dance floor
Showing everybody how
you'd gone beyond your sorrow
No one could hurt you now

love's only good
when you come back from the war

love's only good
when you're back from the war

I'm a slave to the truth
though it's not what I planned

all through the night
there were cries of every creature
and they cried
        o they cried
only the moon
with its vaguely human features
could arise
        above its crying
of the night

if I could speak
if the time would only

if I could cry
I would cry myself a river
and I'd sail, I'd go sailing
through the night

***

make it easy baby
can't pass another test
just spread your blanket on the sand
where both of us can rest

they stopped me in the subway
I didn't have my car
make it easy baby
the shit has got too hard

make it easy baby
and put my soul to rest
I'll even say I love you
if it ain't some kind of test

make it easy baby
don't make the poor boy wait
those subtle
          subtle invitations
that often come too late

if I had a gifted mind
if I had a gifted tongue
still I'd bitch & moan
that I didn't have enough
that I caught too many colds
that I spent a night alone

if I were deep
if I were bright
if I could keep
the Lord in sight
if I didn't have to ask
if I knew my human task
if I had a certain task

if I could win The Purple Heart
before the battle start

don't condemn
anyone to death
before you've had
your coffee

***

To lead a private life
a lonely American marriage
a song on the charts
a house in Greece
the best of drugs
friendly with the maitre d'
in three of four good restaurants
donations to {the television picture}
of a starving child
a private life of exemplary elegance
and humanity

a vegetarian a Scientologist
a patron of the latest revolution
a private life with several ladies
and a highly dependent wife
whatever happened to my private life
whatever happened to my suit of Harris Tweed
and my long Aegean suntan
whatever happened to my place
in the Anthology of English Literature
and here we are with no one but each other
and the tear gas drifting through the trees

and here we are without a family crest
and here we are with plans to build a city
and here we are with killers in our midst
whom we love
whom we depend on
killers whom none of us can trust
and it's late and it's early
    as all the experts say

and all of us are amateurs
   in what we do today

whatever happened to the private life
the poets and the singers promised me

To lead a private life
like a pirate with his knife

***

Paris March 1969

If Kenneth Koch wasn't so funny
   he'd have to carry a gun
because he steals men's wives
and what is worse
     gives them back
complete with assorted old jokes
he tried to prevent me
from discovering the whereabouts
of Terry Southern's ex-wife
     but conscience drove him
to phone up the next day
and apologize
actually I phoned him
and he apologized in passing
I could have waited a long time
for that phone-call

***

Travelogue

the {beefy} burghers of Montreal
elude a humpty-dumpty fall
by climbing not a single wall
or hill or steps or stairs at all

the stables of the King are bare
and his soldiers couldn't care—
the beefy burghers do not dare
to risk eternal disrepair

they did not hear me when I fell
and fractured all my mortal shell
flutes of bone, fine flutes to sell
a skull that rattles like a bell

***

to the young let me say:
I am not sage, rebbe, roshi, guru
I am Bad Example.
to experienced persons
who have characterized my life work
as cheap, superficial, pretentious, insignificant:
        you do not know
        how Right you are

among the whores
there are some of us
who want to make love well
and among {those} these
a few
who do it for nothing

I am a whore
and a junkie.
if some of my songs
made a moment
easier for you,
please remember this.

***

I loved you. I envied you. I thought I had a
right to your company. When that time came I
wasted it in tales of strength and boasting. Your
lovely light has guided me so long.
Sometimes the light of a firefly, sometimes the light of a furnace.

***

and when the ordeal
        that you know and you feel
is truly refined and upheld
we'll meet in the house
        that's prepared for the spouse
of the widowed lord
        of us all

***

I saw her comb her long black hair
and then I loved her jealously
I broke my life in two for her
and she's no good for me

Her {full moon} breasts
        tipped rosy red
O God I love her jealously
She burns my heart she warms my bed
& she's no good for me

***

We go down to the café
on Mount Royal
where they have the records of home
and we spend our quarters to hear
the songs that were born in the sun

and we dance with a twisted handkerchief
through the long nights of snow
and for all the sweet time that a song can last
back to the islands we go

and soon they turn the juke-box off
and there's only five of us left

and we're done with the talking of politics
and the beer is up to our necks
we sing like we sang on the island
when we'd sail up the moonlit steps
and if you could look through the blizzard
you'd see the blood on our lips

Don't forget me Demetra
Don't forget what you know
I'll be coming back with the money
in fifteen years or so

***

Karen's beauty is very great
it lies on her heart like a paperweight
She haunts the edges of her beauty
like a ghost on sentry duty
If beauty is the motherland
she lives on the furthest strand
Her back toward the Capitol
that the pilgrims call so beautiful
She hears them make a joyous sound
but she cannot turn around
The lover's song and the victim's rack
they soar and creak behind her back
Through her beauty many pass
like penitents on broken glass
But once inside there is no cure
for hearts so wounded at the door

Trying to find a place to kneel
between the poets of pain
Trying to find a world to feel
that feels like the world again
My darling says her love is real
then why does she complain

***

    You talk about telling me the truth and then you threaten to write all over my book of poems. Let us put an end to this chatter.
    You expressed some curiosity as to whether I would love you or kill you in response to one of your gestures. I am neither a saint nor a murderer: I do not love and I do not kill. I make love and I tear the wings off flies

***

One more drink
                    for the boys at the bar
I'd tell you all about us
        but I don't know who we are

One more cry
            from the pedal steel guitar

for the war that we lost
for the girl that we wanted
for the man that we double-crossed
all day at the office

for the scout from the major league
who's never gonna spot ya
Get em up, Joe,
            like you did for Frank Sinatra

***

August 2, 1976

I stole your sister for a little ritual that failed
I stole your savior with his hands so firmly nailed
I stole the crescent moon its image in the sea
I stole your roses and your lapis lazuli

I stole the bullets made of silver and your gun
I stole your many gods, I stole the only one
I stole the tower with a woman leaning there
I stole your lover from the ladder of her hair

I crossed the line of reason

I stole your victory handout
and your flimsy Holocaust

I stole the midnight special from the trash
So go to sleep, it's never coming back
I stole your former wife, I had to tell her why
you kept on coming back to say goodbye

I crossed a moat, a high electric fence
I stole your Jews and Gypsies tangled from the trench {tangled in a trench}
I stole your victim [?] memory your holocaust
I have stolen everything you lost

***

For I have been thru many lives
& no one follows me
I am what you were last night
& I am what you'll be

The moment that you track me down
I surrender there
I leave you with a bag of cracks
that you know you must repair

***

You came to me
You wear your widow clothes
I ask who are you mourning for
you say, The man you were before
The man you were before
I loved you

I remember him

Didn't he live
on an island in
the Mediterranean sea
with a mandate from God
to enter the dark

263

Acceptance Address for the Prince of Asturias Award

Your Majesty, Your Royal Highnesses, Excellencies, Members of the Jury, Distinguished Laureates, Ladies and Gentlemen:

It is a great honor to stand here before you tonight. Perhaps, like the great maestro Riccardo Muti, I am not used to standing in front of an audience without an orchestra behind me, but I will do my best as a solo artist tonight.

I stayed up all night last night wondering what I might say to this august assembly. And after I had eaten all the chocolate bars and peanuts in the minibar, I scribbled a few words. I don't think I have to refer to them. Obviously, I am deeply touched to be recognized by the Foundation. But I've come here tonight to express another dimension of gratitude. I think I can do it in three or four minutes—and I will try.

When I was packing in Los Angeles to come here, I had a sense of unease because I've always felt some ambiguity about an award for poetry. Poetry comes from a place that no one commands and no one conquers. So I feel somewhat like a charlatan to accept an award for an activity which I do not command. In other words, if I knew where the good songs came from, I'd go there more often.

I was compelled in the midst of that ordeal of packing to go and open my guitar. I have a Conde guitar, which was made in Spain in the great workshop at Number 7 Gravina Street; a beautiful instrument that I acquired over 40 years ago. I took it out of the case and I lifted it. It seemed to be filled with helium—it was so light. And I brought it to my face. I put my face close to the beautifully designed rosette, and I inhaled the fragrance of the living wood. You know that wood never dies.

I inhaled the fragrance of cedar as fresh as the first day that I acquired the guitar. And a voice seemed to say to me, "You are an old man and you have not said thank you; you have not brought your gratitude back to the soil from which this fragrance arose." And so I come here tonight to thank the soil and the soul of this people that has given me so much—because I know just as an identity card is not a man, a credit rating is not a country. Now, you know of my deep association and confraternity with the poet Federico García Lorca. I could say that when I was a young man, an adolescent, and I hungered for a voice, I studied the English poets and I knew their work well, and I copied their styles, but I could not find a voice. It was only when I read, even in translation, the works of Lorca that I understood that there was a voice. It is not that I copied his voice; I would not dare. But he gave me permission to find a voice, to locate a voice; that is, to locate a self, a self that is not fixed, a self that struggles for its own existence.

And as I grew older I understood that instructions came with this voice. What were these instructions? The instructions were never to lament casually.

And if one is to express the great inevitable defeat that awaits us all, it must be done within the strict confines of dignity and beauty.

And so I had a voice, but I did not have an instrument. I did not have a song.

And now I'm going to tell you very briefly a story of how I got my song.

Because I was an indifferent guitar player. I banged the chords. I only knew a few of them. I sat around with my college friends, drinking and singing the folk songs, or the popular songs of the day, but I never in a thousand years thought of myself as a musician or as a singer.

One day in the early '60s, I was visiting my mother's house in Montreal. The house is beside a park, and in the park there's a tennis court where many people come to watch the beautiful young tennis players enjoy their sport. I wandered back to this park, which I'd known since my childhood, and there was a young man playing a guitar. He was playing a flamenco guitar, and he was surrounded by two or three girls and boys who were listening to him. I loved the way he played. There was something about the way he played that captured me.

It was the way I wanted to play—and knew that I would never be able to play.

And I sat there with the other listeners for a few moments, and when there was a silence, an appropriate silence, I asked him if he would give me guitar lessons. He was a young man from Spain, and we could only communicate in my broken French and his broken French. He didn't speak English. And he agreed to give me guitar lessons. I pointed to my mother's house, which you could see from the tennis court, and we made an appointment; we settled the price.

And he came to my mother's house the next day and he said, "Let me hear you play something." I tried to play something. He said, "You don't know how to play, do you?" I said, "No, I really don't know how to play." He said, "First of all, let me tune your guitar. It's all out of tune." So he took the guitar, and he tuned it. He said, "It's not a bad guitar." It wasn't the Conde, but it wasn't a bad guitar. So he handed it back to me. He said, "Now play."

I couldn't play any better.

He said "Let me show you some chords." And he took the guitar and he produced a sound from the guitar that I'd never heard. And he played a sequence of chords with a tremolo, and he said, "Now you do it." I said, "It's out of the question. I can't possibly do it." He said, "Let me put your fingers on the frets." And he put my fingers on the frets. And he said, "Now, now play." It was a mess. He said, "I'll come back tomorrow." He came back tomorrow. He put my hands on the guitar. He placed it on my lap in the way that was appropriate, and I began again with those six chords—[the] six-chord progression that many, many flamenco songs are based on.

I was a little better that day.

The third day: improved, somewhat improved. But I knew the chords now. And I knew that although I couldn't coordinate my fingers with my thumb to produce the correct tremolo pattern, I knew the chords—I knew them very,

very well by this point. The next day, he didn't come. He didn't come. I had the number of his boarding house in Montreal. I phoned to find out why he had missed the appointment, and they told me that he'd taken his life—that he committed suicide. I knew nothing about the man. I did not know what part of Spain he came from. I did not know why he came to Montreal. I did not know why he stayed there. I did not know why he appeared there in that tennis court. I did not know why he took his life. I was deeply saddened, of course.

But now I disclose something that I've never spoken in public. It was those six chords—it was that guitar pattern that has been the basis of all my songs and all my music.

So now you will begin to understand the dimensions of the gratitude I have for this country. Everything that you have found favorable in my work comes from this place.

Everything, everything that you have found favorable in my songs and my poetry is inspired by this soil.

So I thank you so much for the warm hospitality that you have shown my work, because it is really yours, and you have allowed me to affix my signature to the bottom of the page.

Thank you so much, ladies and gentlemen.

INDEX OF TITLES / *DRAWINGS, FIRST LINES*

271

275